PLAYGR...

Let your creativity flow...

ode
limerick
haiku
rhyme
ball...
my poems

Poems From The UK
Edited by Steve Twelvetree

 Young**Writers**

First published in Great Britain in 2005 by:
Young Writers
Remus House
Coltsfoot Drive
Peterborough
PE2 9JX
Telephone: 01733 890066
Website: www.youngwriters.co.uk

SB ISBN 1 84602 207 X

Foreword

Young Writers was established in 1991 and has been passionately devoted to the promotion of reading and writing in children and young adults ever since. The quest continues today. Young Writers remains as committed to the fostering of burgeoning poetic and literary talent as ever.

This year's Young Writers competition has proven as vibrant and dynamic as ever and we are delighted to present a showcase of the best poetry from across the UK. Each poem has been carefully selected from a wealth of *Playground Poets* entries before ultimately being published in this, our thirteenth primary school poetry series.

Once again, we have been supremely impressed by the overall high quality of the entries we have received. The imagination, energy and creativity which has gone into each young writer's entry made choosing the best poems a challenging and often difficult but ultimately hugely rewarding task - the general high standard of the work submitted amply vindicating this opportunity to bring their poetry to a larger appreciative audience.

We sincerely hope you are pleased with our final selection and that you will enjoy *Playground Poets Poems From The UK* for many years to come.

Contents

Brington CE Primary School, Huntingdon
Oliver Mas (9)   20

Brixton St Mary's CE Primary School, Plymouth
Rebecca Johns (9)   20
Amy Bent (11)   21
Jemma-Anne Kay (10)   21
Matthew Spindley (10)   22
Aimee Dowding (11)   22
Lauren Evans (11)   23
Joshua Hunt (10)   23

Bromesberrow St Mary's CE Primary School, Ledbury
Sam Hart (9)   24
Christopher Prout (10)   24
Alex Bayross (10)   25
Hannah Trigg (10)   25
Chayce Parslow (10)   26

Bushfield Middle School, Milton Keynes
Holly Nealis (11)   26
Joe Bulman (10)   26
Florence Mutlow (10)   27
Laura Beaton (9)   27
Sarah Beth Sheard (10)   28
Rachael Banes (9)   28

Claremont Community Primary School, Blackpool
Jack Royals (8)   28

Crown Primary School, Inverness
Heather McGowan (10)   29

Dobwalls Primary School, Cornwall
Jed Brown (8)   29
Megan Williams   30
Jodie Park (9)   30
Dominic Folland (8)   30
Hazel Scott (9)   31

Georgia Ryder (9)	31
Grace Sutton (9)	31
Jay Miles (9)	32
Emma Roberts (8)	32
William Pounder (9)	33
Emily Lewis (9)	33
Harley Ford (9)	33
Bethany Welch (8)	34
Tyde Dominic (9)	34
Alice Mack (8)	34
Michael Slater (9)	35
Harry Chambers (9)	35

Doonfoot Primary School, Ayr

Kimberley Gibb (11)	36
Nia Clark (11)	36
Eilidh Logan (11)	37
Laura Bryce (11)	37
Raechel McGinn (11)	38
Katie Offer (11)	39
Ruth Swanson (11)	40
Lucy Purdie (11)	41
Lillian Tait (11)	41
Jennifer Gaskell (11)	42
Celine Cairney (11)	43
Stephanie Paton (11)	43
Fraser Cairns (11)	44
Chelsea Deacon (12)	44
David Grant (11)	45
Andrew Rae (12)	45
Paul McKellar (11)	46
Nicole Cain (11)	46
Lucy Porter (11)	47
Louise Turriff (11)	47
Caroline Mack (11)	48
Joanna Hughes (11)	48
Jack Wylie (11)	49
Sophie Steele (11)	49
Oliver Vollam (11)	50
Ross McKeith (11)	50
Shona Norval (11)	51

Christopher Nelson (8)   69
Lewis Paxton-Fear (9)   69
Ella Richardson (9)   70
Oliver Cuss (9)   70

Kingswells School, Aberdeen

Jasmine Gray (11)   71
Hayley Anderson (11)   72
Lisa Murray (12)   72
Sarah Milne (11)   73
Robert Meiklejohn (12)   73
Mikey Christides (11)   74
Amanda Rattray (11)   75
Leoni Forsyth (12)   76
Iain McKay (12)   76
Yasmin Livingstone (11)   77
Callum Hutchinson (11)   77
Jack Ironside (11)   78
Daniel Cowper (11)   79
Daniel Busby (11)   79
Ben Lobban (11)   80
Victoria Moir (11)   80
Drew Milne (11)   81
Rachel Thompson (11)   81
Stephi Quinn (11)   82
Liam Brown (11)   82
Rachel Forsyth (11)   83
Lauren Cursiter (11)   83
Catriona Webster (12)   84

Marybank Primary School, Muir of Ord

Andrew Bell (10)   84

Minster CE Primary School, Minster

Sam Emery (8)   85
Paige Allen (9)   86
Emmylou Hamill (9)   87
Oliver Coleman (8)   88
Daniel Adamson (9)   89
Louise Cooper (9)   90
Sam Cornwall (9)   91

Miskin Primary School, Mountain Ash

Mornington Primary School, Nottingham

Jamie Ball (10)	118
Connor Chettle (11)	118
Jonathan Huggard (11)	119
Victoria Thorpe (11)	120
Rebecca Armstrong (11)	120
Sabrina Akhtar (10)	121
Andrew Jobe (10)	121
Lauren Palin (10)	122
Sophie Cook (10)	122
Hollie Raven (11)	122
Elly Passingham (10)	123
Charlotte Shelbourn (11)	123
Lauren Turner (11)	123
Aidan Southall (11)	124
Ellie Richmond (10)	124
Lucy Stirland (10)	125
Jordan Towers (11)	125
Christopher Churchman (11)	126
Jack Barnes (11)	126
Emmeline Wilcock (10)	127
Tom Guile (11)	127
Tina Bozorgi (10)	128
Daniel Turner (11)	128
Sam Boneham (11)	129
Glen Daley (11)	129
Serena Kaur Johal (11)	130
Natasha Heaps (10)	130
Tevin Sahota (10)	131
Ajay Sohal (11)	131
Sophie Avci (11)	132
Mollie Carberry (10)	133
Reena Dewshi (11)	134
Daniel Pacey (11)	134
Yasmine Zeidan (11)	135
Aneesa Khan (11)	135
Amy Ellison (10)	136

New Gilston Primary School, Leven

Cameron Souter (10)	136
Simon Scott (11)	137
Kirsty Souter (8)	138

Lauren Fisher (7)   155
Jordon Puckey (8)   155
Byron Puckey (8)   155
Megan Tamblyn (8)   155
Joseph Callum Oxley (7)   156
Jonathan Lewis (8)   156
Hayley Alice Bentley (7)   156
Dillon Hooker (8)   156
Chloe Jones (8)   157
Cameron Brooks (8)   157

Redhill Primary School, Derby
Rachel Thompson (7)   157

Red Rose Primary School, Chester-Le-Street
David Oliver (10)   158
Jennifer Walls (10)   158
Holly Neave (10)   159
Robbie Hall (9)   159
Ryan Jefferson (10)   160
Lisa Ryan (10)   160
Victoria Towler (10)   161
Jake Danby (10)   162
Sophie Hodgson (10)   162
Jayne Beveridge (9)   163
Anna Burn (9)   164
Zak Dunster (10)   165
Alastair Usher (10)   165
Sarah Donkin (10)   166
Steven Jamfrey (10)   166
Connor Bell (10)   167
Alex Miller (10)   167
Zak Cordell (10)   168
Rebecca Clarke (9)   169
Jake Henaghan (9)   169
Anthony Beach (9)   170

Richmond Hill School, Luton
Mansoor Ahmed (9)   170
Maddy Ellems (9)   170
Karl Fludgate (9)   171

Connor McLurg (11) 182
Cameron Ramsay (11) 183
Reice MacKale (10) 183
Callum Scott (11) 183
Christopher Black (11) 184
Lisa White (12) 184
Nicole Steadwood (11) 184
Iain Ramsay (12) 185
Rachael Dalgetty (11) 185
Lucy Denholm (12) 185
Bonamy Tetteh-Lartey (10) 186
Samantha Rush (11) 186
Marcos Koulis (11) 187
John Bain (10) 187
Sean Anderson (11) 187

St Teresa's Catholic Primary School, St Helens
Ryan Robinson (10) 188
Michael Atherton (11) 188
Luke James (11) 189
Kayleigh Leyden (11) 189
Emily Hughes (11) 190
Martin Howard (11) 190
Joanna Bebbington (11) 191
Liam Oakshott (11) 191
Emily Talau (11) 192
Jessica Leather (11) 193
Joe Snee (10) 194
Patrick Tobin (11) 194

Sacred Heart RC Primary School, Leigh
Elizabeth McCrory (9) 195
Dylan Alexander (9) 195
Liam Stridgeon (9) 196
Matthew Merwin (11) 196
Louise Pemberton (9) 197
Justin Beacall (11) 197
Jemma Morrissey (9) 198
Molly Marsh (10) 198
Conor McGuinness (9) 199
Hannah Ridley (10) 199

Simona Zivkovska (10)   222
Mohamed Ahmed (10)   222
Atera Rahman (11)   223
Lisa Thi Tran (10)   223

Ticehurst & Flimwell CE Primary School, Wadhurst
Luke Brown (10)   224
Emily Iliffe (10)   224
Jodie Howe (9)   225
Ryan Bell (9)   225
Clarice Wale (10)   226
George Thomas (8)   226
Amy-Lee Fisher (10)   227
Eleanor Sands (9)   227
Aaron Mills (9)   228
Billie-Jean Stacy (9)   228
Jasmine Perry (10)   228
Amber Brooker (10)   229
Joshua Grinham (9)   229
Gemma West (10)   230
Edward Bennett (10)   230

Trawden Primary School, Colne
Charles Winstanley (11)   230

Whitemoor Primary School, St Austell
Laura Hawken (8)   231
Brendan Collings (7)   231
Fiona Hawkey (8)   232
Shakkira Perryman (7)   232
Luke Harby (6)   232
Sadie Firkins (8)   233
Ben Hooper (7)   233
Marcus Reed (7)   233
Steven Mclinden (6)   234
Ebony Uren (7)   234
Lauren Parish (7)   234
Sophie Symons (7)   235
Jowan Dorson (6)   235

The Poems

Sun

The sun is hot.
The sun comes by,
When the sun comes by, it is summer.
When the sun goes down, the moon comes out.
The sun shines bright.
The moon is dark.
The moon sleeps as well
And the sun sleeps too.
The sun is everywhere.
Don't look at the sun for a long time.

Benny Adu-Mensah (8)

Laura

L ovely little girl,
A lways cute and cuddly,
U sually in a whirl,
R eally full of mischief,
A   proper nine-year-old girl.

Laura Gove

The Wind

The wind blows slowly across the sea
It makes the dolphins smile
It helps the fish swim
But the best thing about it is
It makes the sea sing.

Katie Giles

My Baby Sister

My baby sister is nice
She has lovely blue eyes.
I hug her and kiss her
And take care of her.
Some days she can be naughty
And hit me with her toys.
She puts my things in her potty
Then screams and makes a noise.

Kamiylah Watkins-Fogah (5)

Trees

Trees are getting bigger all the time
Trees are changing colour, even mine
Trees are touching the sky
Trees are catching kites flying high
Trees are growing leaves on summer days
Trees are fainting on winter days

Goodbye trees!

Stephan Monfront (9)

I Went For A Ride

I went out to the stable to go on a ride.
There I stood and watched with pride
As my horse glistened in the dawn.
Off I rode to the edge of the sea,
With my dog chasing me gleefully.

Rebecca Mackellar (10)
Ardgour Primary School, Fort William

Summer

Summer crawls
in after spring,
stealing quietly as a moue,
warming days and evenings too,
bees are buzzing around the house.

Summer chases
the spring away,
blossoms sweetly scent the air,
flowers bloom in gardens and wood,
birds are singing without a care.

Summer defended
against Autumn's approach,
hot sun blazed down every day,
baking streets, and people too,
wishing summer would never go away.

Reece MacKay (11)
Ardgour Primary School, Fort William

Autumn

Autumn falls,
silently and unannounced,
chasing away Summer,
painting each leaf and covering the ground,
in a way that calms each sound.

Autumn gallops
along the winding paths,
snatching leaves off the trees,
bullying each animal personally
with a chilly little breeze.

Autumn leaps
through the darkening days,
snarling at its will,
blowing flowers and meadow plants,
a season which will not stay still.

Holly Davidson (11)
Ardgour Primary School, Fort William

Week Of Spring Weather

On Monday warm rain washed through the town
and turned the streets a muddy brown.

Tuesday, winds blew like shooting stars,
rattling windows and shaking cars.

On Wednesday the sun shone bright like gold,
chasing away winter's cold.

Thursday, the hail hit hard
killing all the flowers in the yard.

Friday's frost froze all the lakes,
trapping the feet of seven drakes.

Saturday's skies were blue and clear
making summer seem very near.

On Sunday the sun came back once more,
brightening up the fields and the shore.

Kyle Davidson (9)
Ardgour Primary School, Fort William

Week Of Spring Weather

On Monday the hail came down,
no one walked in the town.

Tuesday, the wind it blew and blew,
in the city and country too.

On Wednesday, the sun came out.
'Spring is here,' so people shout.

Thursday, the sun blazed bright,
kids wore shorts and flew a kite.

On Friday rain rode back to town
soaking plants in the ground.

Saturday's wetness didn't last long,
happy birds began singing their song.

On Sunday it was calm, no rain!
Then the week began again.

Krystie Wright (10)
Ardgour Primary School, Fort William

Week Of Summer Weather

On Monday scorching heat burnt down
and dried up drains all over town.

Tuesday's warmth cheered up the ash, elm
and the other trees in a flash.

On Wednesday bursts of thundery rain
cooled the air once again.

Thursday stood warm and calm,
the sun was bright but did no harm.

Friday's sun singed your ears,
it was strong enough to defrost your tears.

Saturday's sky was bright light blue.
By the lake, flowers grew.

Hot and sticky was Sunday's weather.
So we all went swimming together.

Xavier Hatfield (10)
Ardgour Primary School, Fort William

A Week Of Summer Weather

On Monday brightness swept through the farm.
The scorching heat made mills slow down.

Tuesday the sun-roasted roofs and walls,
melting ice cream on market stalls.

On Wednesday the summer burst through the wood
and busy bees buzzed in a happy mood.

On Thursday over the fields the sun rolled on,
lighting up the world as it shone.

On Friday the sun fastened on to rock,
blazing down on it making it hot.

On Saturday the sky was blue and so light
with not a single cloud in sight.

On Sunday its rays beamed down again,
oh how I wished for a day of rain!

Karen MacAskill (9)
Ardgour Primary School, Fort William

Spring

Spring crawled
through the waiting woods
bringing new life to the trees,
changing dead branches into new
with fresh green leaves.

Spring slipped
through the surrounding fields
turning rotten grass to rich green,
waking up daffodils and daisies too,
so colourful a world.

Spring sprang
down through the countryside,
gardens bloomed, livening everything up,
and people smiled
to see life begin again.

Amber Lawrie (10)
Ardgour Primary School, Fort William

Summer

Summer strolled
through the grass-filled meadows,
flowers swayed calmly.
The sun sat brightly in the sky.
Children frolicked happily.

Summer strode
with the mighty stag,
warming each wood and field,
touching gently the newborn calf,
as all the piglets squealed.

Summer galloped
with people to the beach,
burning gold the backs of men,
roasting every grain of sand.
I remember the summer when I was ten!

David Wright (11)
Ardgour Primary School, Fort William

Gorgeous Sticky Toffee

Brightly my eyes shimmer and shine,
Like silver stars upon a rooftop.
I stare at the Cadbury toffee wrapper,
The two colours of the wrapper blend together beautifully,
Rich gold and shiny purple.
My eyes sparkle like a ruby.
Slithering and sliding, my hand wriggles
Towards the caramel chocolate,
Just like a worm wriggling towards its hole in the earth.
ll pick it up slowly.
Wrinkling the wrapper wildly, I put it towards my ear.
I hear crackling and bubbling, like liquid in a witch's cauldron.
As I open it, it turns, rolls and somersaults like an acrobat.
It tumbles out of the shiny foil wrapper.
Quickly, I pick the éclair up.
I sniff the sticky toffee,
Mmmmm . . .
Signals shoot to my brain and all through my body,
Something good is about to happen.
The sweet goes into my mouth,
Soft, slippery and now mushy,
I bite it.
Chocolate explodes and pours into my mouth
Like the massive tsunami wave.
The toffee shrinks smaller and smaller
Until it's gone completely.
It's not fair!
I wish I had a bag full,
That would be Heaven!
I'm still hungry, but I feel very happy.

Frankie Harrison (9)
Asfordby Hill CP School, Melton Mowbray

Creamy, Dreamy Chocolate

Brightly my eyes glow, wide with excitement
As I look at the shiny gold and purple wrapper.
When I touch it, the wrapper crinkles and
wrinkles like a gun reloading.
My brain senses that something is happening,
I can sense it.
As I pull the wrapper, the hard sweet
twirls and swirls and somersaults.
The gorgeous aroma drifts up my nose.
I pop the ball of caramel into my mouth.
Mmmmmm!
It's amazing!
I cannot believe how it makes me feel.
I feel so excited, I'm in Heaven.
Now it's all gone.
Noooooooo!
I feel so sad. I want another one.
Yum, yum, yummy.

Daniel Kinnersley Smith (8)
Asfordby Hill CP School, Melton Mowbray

Mmmmmm . . .

I look at the shiny wrapper,
I cannot wait to dig my teeth into it.
I cannot imagine what it tastes like until I eat it!
Slowly I pick it up,
I grab the corners and I pull.
The sweet falls out,
I pop it into my mouth.
As I suck, my tongue tosses it around
Then I chomp, chew and tear the hard ball apart.
I suck again,
Slowly it gets smaller and smaller.
My teeth are sticking together.
The sweet becomes tiny.
I swallow it,
It slides down my throat as fast as a rocket.
I feel happy inside.
I wish I had another, because I am famished!

Sally Riley (9)
Asfordby Hill CP School, Melton Mowbray

Butterflies In My Tum

I glance like a mystic hawk stalking its prey.
The swizzling wrapper looks like a multicoloured
vortex of the beyond.
Shining brightly, the wrapper is a gunshot of colour.
As the wrinkly wrapper turns, it crackles and hisses
like a coloured Roman candle.
The heavenly aroma floats up my nose,
my mouth waters like Niagara Falls.
The moment of truth arrives.
I force it into my mouth,
the taste is sensational,
there is no earthly word to describe it.
It is superextraviganza!
I bet no man, animal or creature
has ever experienced this taste.
I nibble, bite and chew.
It slowly disappears,
Only micro-grains of chocolate are left on my tongue.
My mouth now feels like a barren wasteland.
My emotions overcome me.
I run upstairs sobbing,
anxious for another!

Ben Jackson (9)
Asfordby Hill CP School, Melton Mowbray

Cold, Cold Clementine

I dig my nail into the hard, firm skin, tearing large pieces of peel.
I smell it.
The lovely looking peel is like an uncompleted jigsaw.
I am calm but excited looking at it.
It makes my mouth water.
Slowly I put the small segments into my mouth
Wondering what the taste will be.
My mouth mushes it up.
The tangy, bitter taste wakens my mouth
And the sharpness of the fruit alarms my taste buds.
The tongue absorbs the sweet juice,
Swept away from its protection.
I just want more.
Some juice escapes from my mouth,
Like an animal escaping from its cage,
then I swallow.
I realise it is all gone.
I get a piece of kitchen towel,
I wipe my mouth,
Finding bits of that gorgeous clementine.
Slowly I place the peel in the bin,
Wishing I had more.

Oliver Riddell (10)
Asfordby Hill CP School, Melton Mowbray

Caramel Crush

Brightly my eyes glow like a star on a starry night.
It's shiny bright,
It crinkles and wrinkles in my ear, I'm in Heaven.
I pull it, it swirls and twirls,
It smells too gorgeous.
I pop it into my mouth.
As I suck it, it slips. I've got butterflies.
It's sweet and swerves round my mouth, mmm . . .
I gnaw and bite, *chomp!*
Juice splashes out like an erupting volcano.
Mmmmmm . . .
Creamy, dreamy.
I feel sad, but now I've got a new one.
It tastes really nice,
I want ten thousand more.
Mmmmmm.

Jack Handley (9)
Asfordby Hill CP School, Melton Mowbray

Young Writers - Playground Poets Poems From The UK

Mmmmm!

Brightly my eyes sparkle, like stars at night in the black sky.
They start to gleam and glow like candles.
The wrapper crackles in my ear,
It makes me feel so excited.
The aroma floats up into my nostrils.
I look at the hard brown éclair.
Quickly I pop it into my watering mouth.
Mmmmm . . .
It's delicious, gorgeous, especially in the middle.
I'm chomping, sucking and licking the sweet.
It's now so small.
Oh no, it's disappeared.
I feel so greedy, like a starving pig
That has had no food for a year!
I'm so greedy that I want another one.
I feel so happy inside, just like I have won the lottery!

Kimberley Batsford (9)
Asfordby Hill CP School, Melton Mowbray

Chocolate Éclair, Yum!

Brightly my eyes shine, like stars in the bright sky.
Glittering, shining, glowing, beaming.
I pick it up and hold it to my ear.
It crackles like lightning!
Scrunchy!
I'm so tempted - but no, not yet!
It twirls and somersaults like an acrobat!
Crinkle, crinkle.
I smell the sweet chocolate.
It smells like chocolate cake!
The sweet aroma floats up my nostrils.
Mmmmmmmmm!
I smell caramel!
I pull the éclair to my lips,
I pop it into my mouth as fast as a bullet!
Suck, suck, suck, my lips go.
Mmmmmmmmm!
I taste caramel!
Oh no, the sweet is stuck to my teeth!
Argh!
That's better, my tongue got it off!
Here come my teeth!
Devour, crush, rip, tear, and destroy!
Chocolate explodes out!
Bye-bye chocolate!
I feel full and satisfied!

Chloe Davison (9)
Asfordby Hill CP School, Melton Mowbray

My Alphabetical Friends

A is for Alex who likes ants,
B is for Ben who loves playing bowling,
C is for Cara who is a cat lover,
D is for Danielle who loves dogs,
E is for Emma, she likes elephants,
F is for Frank, he likes fighting,
G is for Gina who likes giraffes,
H is for Hayley who likes being happy,
I is for Isabel who hates insects,
J is for Jessica who likes the jungle,
K is for Kate who likes koalas,
L is for Lauren who likes leopards,
M is for Maxine, she loves music,
N is for Natalie, she loves to natter,
O is for Olivia, she likes owls,
P is for Phillippa, she hates ponies,
Q is for Quentin, he likes questions,
R is for Rachel, she loves rabbits,
S is for Sophie who likes singing,
T is for Tina, she likes to talk,
U is for Ursula who likes the Underworld,
V is for Vicky, she likes the violin,
W is for Wendy, she loves wolves,
X is for Xanthia who loves Xmas,
Y is for Yvonne who likes yellow,
Z is for Zoe who likes zebras.

Natalie Thomas (11)
Birstwith CE (Controlled) Primary School, Harrogate

The Powerful Leader

By the pole of Witchee Woochee,
By the biggest green forest,
Stood the big brown bear, Totlie,
Mother of the sun Totlie.

Dark behind it stood the wigwam,
Rose the tall imposing wigwam,
Rose the point with colours on it.
Bright before it beat the bear,
Beat the brown and growling bear,
Beat the threatening, powerful bear.

Ella Whitwam (9)
Blue Coat CE Primary School, Wotton-under-Edge

Hiawatha

By the hill son a winter's morning
Sat the little Hiawatha,
Heard the whooshing of the pine trees,
Heard the howling of the wind.
'Sounds of comfort, words of the forest,'
Smiled the gentle Indian babe.

Isabelle Ramsay (8)
Blue Coat CE Primary School, Wotton-under-Edge

Our Hero

St George, St George, the best in the land,
Fought the dragon with a sword in his hand.
The dragon let out a big ball of fire,
That St George certainly did not admire.
His breath was revolting and he showed no fear,
But St George killed with one blow of his spear.

Tom Cullum (8)
Blue Coat CE Primary School, Wotton-under-Edge

Hazzooba, The Indian Chief

By the mountains of Natchoo-Nooba,
By the wondrous statue of light,
Stood the totem of Hazzooba,
Mother of the sun, Hazzooba.

Dark behind it rose the woods,
Rose the woods of paralysing pine cones.
Trees of doom, wonder and luck,
Roaring fires of spirits and phantoms,
Beating, spitting, hissing phantoms.

There the old and wise Nassebo
Nursed the little baby boy,
Hugged him, rocked him in his cradle,
Lay him down on moss upon snow,
Sleeping calmly on moss and snow.

Joe Penaliggon (8)
Blue Coat CE Primary School, Wotton-under-Edge

The Indian Princess

By the forest of Switchy Swooney,
By the shimmering deep blue sea,
Stood the shelter of Nokomis,
Daughter of the moon Nokomis.

On the field this spring morning
Sat the little cradled baby,
Heard the swaying of the pine trees,
Heard the scratching of the bushes,
Sounds of music, words of wonder.
'Daughter of the moon,' they called,
'Daughter of the moon,' she gurgled.

Emma Chalmers (9)
Blue Coat CE Primary School, Wotton-under-Edge

St George

Saint George is dead, he's buried and gone,
He slayed the dragon and now there's none.
23rd of April we must never forget, for it's St George's Day,
Though we never met.

Beth Milner & Alice MacKinnon (9)
Blue Coat CE Primary School, Wotton-under-Edge

I Was Playing On My Computer

I was playing on my computer
When it crashed.
So I went downstairs and
Threw it in the trash.
I'm so bored now,
What should I do?
I know,
Go to the zoo.

Oliver Mas (9)
Brington CE Primary School, Huntingdon

Fear

I think fear is small and mousy,
Scared of . . .
Scared of what?
Scared of . . .
Everything!

I think fear is cold and hard like ice.
Fear, I reckon, is making us scared.
Fear is scared.
Fear is small.
Fear is mousey and cold!

Rebecca Johns (9)
Brixton St Mary's CE Primary School, Plymouth

Fears Of Height

I stare down upon the Earth,
I think of nothing but heights,
I suddenly remember my fear,
My fear of the dreaded heights.

The height I see is frightening,
I want to cry out aloud,
I want to conquer my fear,
But instead I make no sound.

The edges of the rocks are sharp
And there they stay,
I take a step back and wish,
I wish I could fly away.

I go and shelter beneath the trees,
But I go back to the height,
I suddenly conquer my fear,
And step off the edge with delight.

Amy Bent (11)
Brixton St Mary's CE Primary School, Plymouth

Fear

I fear a man who creeps in the dark,
I fear a man whose laugh is like a bark.
I fear a man who boasts and gloats,
I fear a man who has only black coats.

I fear a man who cries in the night,
I fear a man who can't help but fight,
I fear a man who is freaky and scary,
I fear a man who is ever so hairy.

I fear a man whose name is unknown,
I fear a man who has no home,
I fear a man who has bad breath,
I fear a man who can always sense death.

Jemma-Anne Kay (10)
Brixton St Mary's CE Primary School, Plymouth

Hell

In Hell there's evil.
It's hot like a burning, smoking, steaming fire.
It's like a volcano shouting and firing balls,
Like a steam train hooting down the track.
There's anger shooting and hooting and booting,
There's devils piking and spiting and kicking,
There's death and anger,
There's bullying and booting,
There's red, runny, hot, dribbling blood,
There's holes which are like jumping out of a devil plane,
The devils have big, black, dribbly teeth,
There's spikes and thorns which are as sharp as a knife,
Red blood and terror.

Matthew Spindley (10)
Brixton St Mary's CE Primary School, Plymouth

My Cat, Rolly

M y cat is cute and soft,
Y ou can stroke him, he won't mind.

C arry him, he loves it.
A ttacking all the time.
T errorising and lazy.

R olly is amazing,
O ver and over he rolls,
L oving and sweet he is,
L ying all around the house.
Y ou have never seen a cat like Rolly.

Aimee Dowding (11)
Brixton St Mary's CE Primary School, Plymouth

The Dungeon

Awake in a dampened dungeon,
A shocking sight I saw,
A mingled, mangled body
Lying on the floor.

I got out of my manky bed,
I heard a crunching sound,
I'd stepped upon a pile of bones
Dumped upon the ground.

I looked around and felt the floor,
When all o' a sudden I felt,
A cold and bumpy object,
A vast and rusty wrench.

I opened up the iron door
To flee that terrible place,
I stepped out of my dungeon cell,
And left without a trace.

Awake in a dampened dungeon,
A shocking sight I saw,
A mingled, mangled body
Lying on the floor.

Lauren Evans (11)
Brixton St Mary's CE Primary School, Plymouth

Love, It Is . . .

Birds tweeting in the morning,
The sun at night setting,
It is lovely.
The fields glistening and
Frosty in the sun,
It is lovely.
The sun shining on the tree,
The shadows,
It is lovely.

Joshua Hunt (10)
Brixton St Mary's CE Primary School, Plymouth

Don't Tell

Don't tell, I threw my passport in the sea
when I was on holiday in Spain.

Don't tell, I wrote on the walls at school
and said it was Dennis.

Don't tell, I made my dog a spaceship
and sent him to visit Pluto.

Don't tell, I stole my sister's tickets
to go and see Busted's last concert.

Don't tell, I pulled out Bart and Santa's Little Helper from the TV
and made them a little den under my bed.

Don't tell, I caught a chicken
and taught it to do the tango.

Don't tell, I took some lightning from the sky
and used it to cut my sandwiches.

Sam Hart (9)
Bromesberrow St Mary's CE Primary School, Ledbury

The Dusty Computer

Breathing computer dust
The cupboard in the empty room
Had nowhere to go.
The firm, hard door of the cupboard
Spotted the peanuts of pencil scratchings,
The school was held in a leaded circle of trees.

Christopher Prout (10)
Bromesberrow St Mary's CE Primary School, Ledbury

Death Of The Leader

And the war went on
And the clock kept ticking
And the blood still spilling
And touch of death still kicking.

Chains all locked and bolted,
Held him to the wall,
With his eye on the window,
Watching his country fall.

Chorus

Then a bright idea,
Came into his mind,
He banged his head on the wall
And his life became blind.

Chorus

Now nothing was to fight for,
Stop did the war,
But today if you look closely,
You see the blood on the floor.

Chorus.

Alex Bayross (10)
Bromesberrow St Mary's CE Primary School, Ledbury

What School Objects Do

Dictionary popped pencils,
Computer whizzed words,
Chairs pinched people,
Tables juggled jugs,
Clocks bashed books
And the bell unleashes learners.

Hannah Trigg (10)
Bromesberrow St Mary's CE Primary School, Ledbury

The Blue Haze

The blue haze of the bumpy cough
Wafted across Chris' computer,
The leaded pencils laughed at the soft trees,
Inside we looked unhappily out of the window
At the wood.

Chayce Parslow (10)
Bromesberrow St Mary's CE Primary School, Ledbury

Corners

When I look around the playground is full
Every corner, every doorway, full
Noise everywhere filling the air
I always stand in the quiet corner of the playground
It's always quiet
Then a smiling face comes from the playground
And adds me to their puzzle

*(It's a puzzle, the noise is the colour and the
Fullness the picture, the quietness is the missing piece.)*

Holly Nealis (11)
Bushfield Middle School, Milton Keynes

Football In The Playground

Well, football in the playground is quite a dirty game
There's people who will really foul
And some who use their hands
But also people never pass and lose it straight away
And the staff don't know much about footie
So it's like this every day
But hey, hey it's Bushfield, everything's OK.

Joe Bulman (10)
Bushfield Middle School, Milton Keynes

So Many Friends

I don't really like going out to play,
But when I get out it's such fun!
There's Ellie, two Jordans, Miriam and Hana,
Oh! We love playing out in the sun!

We don't have a climbing frame, swings or a slide,
But we still seem to enjoy!
There's two Laurens, Sophia, Imran and Mia!
Oh! Let us all jump for joy!

There are lots of games to choose from,
We make up new ones each day!
There's Beth, April, Sarah and Jenn!
Stop! There goes the whistle,
The end of break for today!

Florence Mutlow (10)
Bushfield Middle School, Milton Keynes

Teachers Won't Play!

It's not fair
They won't play
Maybe they don't care
But hopefully it will be one day.

They can play tennis
Or watch Dennis the Menace
Or maybe tug of war
Or mow the lawn.

They could have a big fight
Or fly a kite
Maybe some parachuting
Or do some skipping.

Laura Beaton (9)
Bushfield Middle School, Milton Keynes

Playground

P laying children
L aughing games
A lways busy climbing frame
Y oungsters crowding
G oing swell
R eaching up
O ver as well
U nder too if you can
N ever seen to fall somehow
D own again, bell is ringing.

Playground empty, lessons now.

Sarah Beth Sheard (10)
Bushfield Middle School, Milton Keynes

My Feelings

When we go out to play
It's like the start of a new day.
But still it's hard to know what's coming,
Whether you'll be crying or running.
But still it's the brighter part
Not having to worry about maths or art.

Rachael Banes (9)
Bushfield Middle School, Milton Keynes

Happiness

Happiness is like a pinky colour like a flamingo.
It sounds like a garden full of playful animals
It's a kind, calm, sweet taste.
It smells like a calm, happy smell.

Jack Royals (8)
Claremont Community Primary School, Blackpool

The Kids On Mum's Birthday!

'Mum he did that.'
'Mum *she* did this.'
'Oh dear, oh dear,' said Mum.
'I thought birthdays were meant to be bliss!'
Mum stood and thought for quite a while and then at last,
'Oh yes, I've got it, hip hip hooray!
Why don't you go out and play!'
'What? With him? Not on your nelly.
I'm going to go and watch the telly!'
'But that's not fair!'
'Well you can watch it later.
Why don't you go and fix your hair?'
'Fine then I will.'
'OK that's settled.'
'But what about Bill?'
'Bill! Bill! Who's Bill?'
'Why, he's my *new* best friend.'
'Argh,' shouted Mum,
'These kids are going to drive me round the bend!'

Heather McGowan (10)
Crown Primary School, Inverness

Senses

It feels like a dusty blunt sword,
It smells like powerful plastic,
It looks like an upside down busy road painted white,
It tastes like spring water straight from the ground,
It sounds like people clapping with steel
Fiercely
I'm describing a white ruler.

Jed Brown (8)
Dobwalls Primary School, Cornwall

Cats And Kittens

He stumbles
His calls pierce the air
She howls back and sniffs the grass
The kitten lies down wet and in despair
He lies down to take a nap in a fluffy mass
He wakes up on hay
His mum with him
She miaows and licks her kitten
He sees the water bucket full to the rim
She knows it's him
Because of the white mittens.

Megan Williams
Dobwalls Primary School, Cornwall

Puppies And Dogs

Puppies barking all around
Dogs barking all around
Go, go dogs, go away, leave me alone
Go, go puppies, go away, leave me alone.

Jodie Park (9)
Dobwalls Primary School, Cornwall

Ship

It sounds like thunder with a thousand squeaking mice
It feels hard and old
It looks like an old Atlantic steamer
What did it do?
Carry cargo and people across the Atlantic Ocean.

Dominic Folland (8)
Dobwalls Primary School, Cornwall

My Kitten

A tabby and white kitten
Licking the pan for milk
Curls up on a warm, soft pillow
Chases the chickens all day
A tabby and white kitten
Scratches and bites and plays with toys
It is tabby and white and playful
Until she sleeps on your pillow
It is like a velvet cushion purring all night.

Hazel Scott (9)
Dobwalls Primary School, Cornwall

Wonder

Standing in the moonlight
I watch the whistling trees
In my head I think of what we will do at noon
Will she come and ride me
Or will I be alone?
Please don't let that be!

Georgia Ryder (9)
Dobwalls Primary School, Cornwall

My Secret

I have a secret very deep and dark
When you go into the woods
And move a certain piece of bark,
You will find yourself in a world of pixies
Pitch-black and dark.

Grace Sutton (9)
Dobwalls Primary School, Cornwall

The Duel

The duel is on.
The duellists draw.
Leogun is summoned.
He roars and roars.

Then one duellist
Starts to frown,
The other summons
And plays one card face down.

The first duellist draws again.
He summons Dark Magician.
Then Leogun attacks
But he's changed to defence position.

Then, Dark Magician attacks.
The duel has ended its competition.

Jay Miles (9)
Dobwalls Primary School, Cornwall

In The Moonlight

I gallop in the moonlight
The moon shows me the way
My shadow trails behind me
The freedom I feel to gallop in the moonlight.

The wind whistles through my mane
My tail swishes from side to side
The cool breeze makes me feel alive.

In the quietness of the night
My hooves go clipperty-clop
The owl hoots to say goodnight
Another moonlight has come to an end.

Emma Roberts (8)
Dobwalls Primary School, Cornwall

The Amazon Rainforest

It can be seen from space
It gleams in tropical sunlight like a green sea
Its animals are weird and wonderful
As they fly and scuttle around
The plants smell sweet like honey
Dripping from the hive.

The river rushes as piranhas look for scraps
The natives dash between the trees
Looking out for a snack
While explorers look frantically for El Dorado
The city of gold hoping to become rich.

William Pounder (9)
Dobwalls Primary School, Cornwall

The Sea

The sea can be calm, the sea can be bare,
The sea can be lonely with nobody there.
The sea gleams red as a rose,
It also has feelings that nobody knows.

The sea can be angry the sea can be tough,
The sea can be happy the sea can be rough.
The sea can be fun like a bouncing trampoline,
But sometimes this rough sea can be extremely mean.

Emily Lewis (9)
Dobwalls Primary School, Cornwall

Animals

Bongos bravely battle
Cheetahs chase the scared cattle
The fanged vampires frighten frogs
The beautiful butterflies land on bogs.

Harley Ford (9)
Dobwalls Primary School, Cornwall

The Chipmunk

The chipmunk, brown and white
Scurrying in the dark
Will he get a fright?
When the dog starts to bark
When the wind starts to blow
The chipmunk hurries inside its home
Up to bed off you go
Go quickly now please don't moan.

Bethany Welch (8)
Dobwalls Primary School, Cornwall

Tiny Spotted Black Ant

A tiny spotted black ant
Creeping on the ground
He looks lost never to be found
Tiny spotted black ant
Creeping on the ground
Searching for his colony
Never to be found.

Tyde Dominic (9)
Dobwalls Primary School, Cornwall

My Rabbit

My rabbit hops
Jumps and runs
My rabbit feels
Like a cloud in the sky
My rabbit looks sweet
Soft like a cuddly teddy bear
My rabbit makes me feel warm.

Alice Mack (8)
Dobwalls Primary School, Cornwall

The Savannah Part Two

(Inspired by the Wildlife Trust Foundation)

G azelle is galloping in the morning breeze
A ntelope having a morning drink
Z ebra edging towards the waterhole
E lephants eating large leaves
L ong horns spotting a pack of hyenas
L ions taking over the waterhole for food and drink
E lephants' young eating the lower branches.

Z ebra running from a leopard
E lephants finding another spot
B aboons having a play fight
R abbits hopping to their holes and their young
A nts scuttling to the nest.

Michael Slater (9)
Dobwalls Primary School, Cornwall

The River Flows

As the river flows, the kingfisher goes
To catch some fish for a tasty dish,
Yet there is more wildlife down by the stream
For stream flows into lake and there is a team
A flock more like Canada geese flying
Carry with them all the peace . . .
In the world of caring caring and sharing -
But there are more than flying creatures
There are fruit like plums and peaches
But not all nature must come to an end
It can't go straight
It must turn a bend.

Harry Chambers (9)
Dobwalls Primary School, Cornwall

The Night, The Stars And The Moon

Night is like a wolf, howling in the sky,
The trees all sway and whistle, I just wonder why?
Maybe it's the winter breeze that makes night act so strange,
But when I wake up in the morning,
There's a blazing sun staring up at me.
What happened to night? I don't know,
Where's the dark night sky that's the colour of coal?

Look at that star, look at that diamond,
Just up there, sitting on the black velvet sky,
All of them dotted about everywhere.
Look at that one! Isn't it cool?
Winking at me in that black whirlpool.
Stars like diamonds, stars like crystals
Dozens of stars twinkling at me.

I see the moon, the moon sees me,
It follows me about in the dead of night.
Big and round, cool and bright,
It glows, it's a big light bulb
In the middle of the sky.
I like the moon and the moon likes me.

Kimberley Gibb (11)
Doonfoot Primary School, Ayr

Black

Black whispers in the darkness
It is a pool of emptiness
Black fills you with memories
Black is the past
It is a mask of secrecy
Black is loneliness that comes at night
It tastes thick and heavy like tar
Black is the touch of a deadly sword
Black surrounds you with peacefulness
And enhances your thoughts.

Nia Clark (11)
Doonfoot Primary School, Ayr

Standing Up For Yourself!

I'm just a black person playing fair
They all stop in the street, give me horrible looks and stare.
With these looks of hatred, I feel so depressed
Nothing wrong with me, I'm the same as the rest!

I'm just a black person playing fair
The whites are so nasty, it's like my skin colour's rare
I feel so dismal, the blacks really should protest
This is not fair, the whites think they're best!

I'm just a black person playing fair
The whites just don't really care
I'll stand up to them, say what's right
I'll stop this without a fight!

I'm just a black person playing fair
Don't look at me, look over there
My life's the same, I eat, sleep and work
Whites please stop this and don't be such a jerk!

Eilidh Logan (11)
Doonfoot Primary School, Ayr

Prejudice

I wish I could be white
To stop this black and white prejudice fight,
We are all the same there's no one to blame,
It's a shame as life's unreasonable.

Black people are pressured
And get a bad name,
I think it's a sin that I have to hide in a bin
When a white person goes by.

My life is like a washing machine, tumbling around.
Oh help! Please explain, I'm frightened of life,
Please take away the pain,
I would like to be white!

Laura Bryce (11)
Doonfoot Primary School, Ayr

Life In The Night Sky

Moon

The moon is up there
And I am down here,
It doesn't look too far,
Why neither does that star!
I'll reach up high,
Up into the dark sky
And I'll catch the moon
In my fishing net so I can say,
Last night it was the moon that I met
But the problem you see,
Is it keeps running away from me,
Even though it looks so still
But one day I'll catch the moon,
I will, I will, I will!

Stars

What are they, those diamonds in the sky?
What are they, those lights upon the dark they lie?
They stare at me like sparkling eyes,
Are they spies?
Are they near me or are they near Mars?
I know what they are, they're *stars!*

Night

As the night creeps in,
The day creeps out,
As the light creeps out,
The dark creeps in,
I've been told
It's dark and it's ice cold,
When there is no light,
We know it's night!

Raechel McGinn (11)
Doonfoot Primary School, Ayr

Night

Night is a smothering black blanket,
Choking out all light.
Night warps our imagination,
Into horror stories and fright!

Night hides all good and bright things,
Night creeps around in the dark.
Night makes a dog sound frightening,
When all it does is bark.

The moon is just a hole in the blanket,
Letting in a small chink.
The moon stops it being so scary
And makes you stop and think.

The moon is a bright beacon,
Guiding the way in the night.
The moon casts some light on the matter
And stops you from getting a fright.

Stars are flecks of diamonds,
Scattered in the sky,
Stars can guide us north,
All those dots, way up high.

Stars are there to help us,
Help us find our way.
Stars are always there at night
And always gone by day.

Katie Offer (11)
Doonfoot Primary School, Ayr

That Girl

That girl over there doesn't like me
And I don't know why
Maybe it's because I'm not rich
Or wear designer clothes.

I don't know why.

My only friend thinks something else
That she doesn't like the way I laugh
Or walk or talk
It could be that.

I feel like I've been hit
With a thousand knives
The girl took my only friend away
Now she hates me too and I don't know why.

I've got an idea
I'm going to talk to her
And find out the thing
That she doesn't like about me.

I'm finding out

She told me
That I am weird and mysterious
And look ugly and horrible.
She turned away.

I grabbed my friend's hand
And took her away
We are friends again
I am happy.

The girl still doesn't like me
I don't care
I'm just me and
That's the way I'll always be.

Ruth Swanson (11)
Doonfoot Primary School, Ayr

My Special Colours

Pink is my favourite colour
It's the colour of my skin
It is the colour of candyfloss
And makes me bright when dim.

Red is the colour when I scrape my knee
It is the colour of poppies
In the new spring blowing around
Red is the colour of anger
That blushes in my cheeks.

Blue is the colour of the relaxing sky
The colour of water
The colour when I cry.

Yellow is the colour of the blazing sun
The colour of Livingston
Fans shouting, 'We're number one.'

Lucy Purdie (11)
Doonfoot Primary School, Ayr

Night, Stars And Aliens

The night hides during the day
And when it's dark it comes out to play.
All during the night it's silent and cold,
The dark night sky is really black and bold.

At night the man in the moon comes out,
He jumps for joy and laughs and shouts.
In the evening he livens the dark sky
And in the morning he says bye bye.

The scientists must have discovered aliens by now,
I wonder where they are?
Maybe Mars, Pluto, Mercury or Venus
But wherever they are I thank you for
The distance between us!

Lillian Tait (11)
Doonfoot Primary School, Ayr

Emotions Merge With Colours

Red is the colour of anger and fury,
A bitter fire burning with fuming rage.

Silver is a beautiful sadness full of lonely ghosts,
A mournful grief that's always there,
Shimmering tears rolling down a painful face.

Gold is an unforgettable glinting happiness,
A star that's always shining in the heavens above,
The colour of childhood and memories passing by.

Pink is the colour of love and peace,
A lovely feeling, full of happiness.
A calm, swaying, wonderful world,
Waiting quietly.

Orange is a colour that's out of this world,
A crazy, mad feeling of colourful things,
A bright, funny place full of laughter and games.

Black is the colour of daydreaming and faraway worlds,
A distracting place that catches your eyes
And takes you into space with supersonic speed.

Yellow is full of fantastic excitement and eagerness,
That pirouettes in a whizzing vortex.
A funny, wild feeling zooming inside yourself,
Waiting to escape.

Blue is a mysterious sadness full of depression and tears,
A place of gloomy and dull surroundings,
Waiting in a calm and unstirred silence.

Purple is a colour of courage and wisdom,
A bright purple light lighting up knowledge and understanding,
A confident feeling of intelligence and judgement.

Emotions can merge with colours,
Depending on how you are feeling.

Jennifer Gaskell (11)
Doonfoot Primary School, Ayr

Dishonesty

Why is it always 'Why can't we win?'
Why do people not understand?
What does it matter the colour of skin?
Why am I having to ask all these questions?
I just do not understand people's intentions.

The world was once a beautiful place,
But soon after that came almost an end to the human race,
Even if black skin is different from white,
I still don't think it is right.

Where is the love?
Why do people not see that peace needs to come from
                                              up above?
People need to fight for freedom now
And all I want to know is how to stop wars
So please someone tell me how!

Celine Cairney (11)
Doonfoot Primary School, Ayr

Friendship!

Friendship is a warm summer's day
And sounds like laughter and fun.
Friendship is a wonderful dance of happiness
And looks like the bright sun gleaming in the window.

Friendship feels like tinkling water around my feet
And makes you feel like you're high in the heavens.
Friendship is in the shape of a loving heart
And is a pocket of hope and honesty.

Friendship tastes like sugary candyfloss
And is a precious box of delicate petals.

Stephanie Paton (11)
Doonfoot Primary School, Ayr

My Colours

Blue is the colour of the clear, cloudless sky,
A calm flowing waterfall, trickling into the sea.
My bright, blue eyes glistening in the sun,
Blue is also a calm and cooling colour.
It is sapphire, a great big gem,
Bluebells, blowing in the cool morning breeze.

Green is the colour of the trees, bending in the wind,
The soft, smooth grass, tickling my chin.
A big green balloon rising high in the bright blue sky,
The little, tiny caterpillar crawling on the leaf.
Green is also ivy, climbing up the wall,
It is mint ice cream, melting on my tongue.

Red is the colour of strawberries, being made into fruit salad,
Poppies blossoming in gardens full of flowers.
Scorching hot lava, bubbling in a volcano,
Red is also fire, burning down a building.
A beautiful butterfly, flying in the breeze,
It is also the colour of rubies, gleaming in the light.

Fraser Cairns (11)
Doonfoot Primary School, Ayr

The Sky At Night

Night is a dark room with all lights turned off.
The clouds are not white anymore.
They are now fading away as a fluffy shadow.
Night is between sunset and sunrise.
It is when sleepy humans lay asleep in their beds.
Night swallows everything in its sight.

The moon moans as it has been woken up by the sun.
When it's his time to do his duty as the moon.
The moon is like a white juicy apple, resting on a cloud.
Sometimes the cloud decides to take over the moon,
Which makes half moon.

Chelsea Deacon (12)
Doonfoot Primary School, Ayr

The Wonders Of The Night

Night swallows up the sky with nothing else to see,
It can't catch you in your bedroom,
So that's where you want to be.
Night is like a black moaning tomb,
So watch out because it could be waiting round the corner.

Planets go round the sun moaning and groaning,
They are always trying to show off with all their colours,
If I were a scientist I'd find it boring,
They're as big as the sun and as small as Russia,
Planets are all different sizes.

Stars sing a melody to put us to sleep
And march around our solar system,
They look as nice as diamond to keep
And are fantastic!

David Grant (11)
Doonfoot Primary School, Ayr

My Teams

Rangers and Celtic are equally the same
They come from the same country and play the same game
But I'll say this now and I'll say this aloud
These teams don't get on for now
I'm a Rangers fan I've been to their games
But this team Celtic they're a bit of a pain
After a match there are usually fights
Smashing each other this usually happens at night
My team means a lot to me I'm sure it does to them the same
But why is there fighting after the games?
My friend Johnny he couldn't care less
He doesn't like football, nevertheless
He's so free-minded and very calm
From the tip of his toes to the palm of his hand
Johnny's a model we could admire!

Andrew Rae (12)
Doonfoot Primary School, Ayr

Paint Box

Red is anger
It is blood spilling from an open wound
It is a juicy apple ready for picking
Red is July

Blue is sadness
It is a rainy day with horrible weather
It is the ocean beyond a deserted beach
Blue is January

Yellow is laughter
It is the blazing sun on a summer's day
It is flames dancing in the fireplace
Yellow is August

Green is guilt
It is a pear almost ripened
It is the open countryside
Green is September

Black is hatred
It is a burglar stealing through the night
It is a black cat scampering across the road
Black is November.

Paul McKellar (11)
Doonfoot Primary School, Ayr

Night

The night sky is a deep dark forest.
Trees whimpering in the dark.
It feels like day will never come back.

The moon on its full beam,
Sucking into its mystical dream.
It shines in the black night sky.

The stars stare at you with their scary eyes,
Poisoning you with their evil lies
As they float about the dark night sky.

Nicole Cain (11)
Doonfoot Primary School, Ayr

They Are Just The Same

The colour of their skin
Doesn't mean they're not nice
Black and white are the same

It is not what they look like
It's what is inside
They might do different things
But still do the same games

Just because they're black
Doesn't mean they're different
They go in town, ride on bikes
They are just the same

They have two eyes
And one nose
Red blood inside

There is no difference
We are the same.

Lucy Porter (11)
Doonfoot Primary School, Ayr

Racism

Racism is a thing of the past,
There really is no difference.
Don't do it,
Don't make it last.

Blacks and whites are just the same,
What do you see wrong with them?
Black and white are just colours,
Don't discriminate it only generates hate.

Whites are no better,
The colour of skin shouldn't change a thing.
Don't hide away,
You're the same on the inside.

Louise Turriff (11)
Doonfoot Primary School, Ayr

Night Sky

At night the trees whisper their secrets,
Leaves cry as they fall to their deaths from the trees,
The stars fight their way through the darkness,
So when you look at them they are smiling with glee.

The moon prowls out from its dark cave,
Shining in the night sky it moans like the whistling wind,
Overtakes the sun trying to be brave
And when it turns to dawn the moon hides again.

An army of stars march out to guide sleeping Earth,
The stars stay busy all night long,
While the shooting stars fly to their holiday in the north of Perth
And the stars guide us to sleep with a Christmas song.

Caroline Mack (11)
Doonfoot Primary School, Ayr

The Starry Sky

The moon prowls out of his dark cave,
His eyebrows down, his face grave,
He looks around at his slaving stars,
The comets speeding like zooming cars.

The stars beg him to let them go free,
Whilst they guard over Earth as we can see,
In their silver suits they march around,
Never to touch our Earth's ground.

The night creeps in and blocks out the sun,
Feeling like it's draining out all the fun,
How do we know that day will come back?
We rely on the stars shining out of the black.

Joanna Hughes (11)
Doonfoot Primary School, Ayr

Night

Night takes a black sheet and spreads it over the sky,
It lures you into its dark world,
Night is a black carpet covering the Earth,
It whispers quietly to the wary trees,
Night switches off day with a frightening laugh.

The moon escapes from its dark sheet of black,
It is a king with stars as slaves,
It swallows up the darkness of the night,
It is as white as snow,
The moon fights away the darkness.

Stars fight their way out of the dark night sky,
They are an army protecting the sleeping Earth,
Stars are bullets being shot from a gun,
They wink at you with beady eyes,
Stars worship the bright moon.

Jack Wylie (11)
Doonfoot Primary School, Ayr

There Really Is No Difference!

There really is no difference,
Whether you're black or white.
Just to be very honest I really don't think it's right!

But just for now close your eyes and think,
What it would be like to be a different colour from everyone else,
Yes, I know you wouldn't like it.

So now you know there really is no difference,
Between them, you and I,
So it just shows that you shouldn't judge people
Before you even know them,
Because inside you feel as if you can cry!

Sophie Steele (11)
Doonfoot Primary School, Ayr

Yellow

Yellow is a banana,
Dropping from a tree.
It is the hot sun,
Shining in the sky.
Little baby chicks
Scampering around.
Yellow is the centre of a daisy,
It is the colour of a winner's medal
Gleaming in the sun.
Yellow, it is the month of June,
The season of summer.
Yellow fills you with joy
On a bright summer's day.
Yellow is a candle
Lighting up the room
Until it dies to an ember.

Oliver Vollam (11)
Doonfoot Primary School, Ayr

The Night Sky

Night swallows everything it sees,
It eats everything whole,
The midnight trees start whispering,
The sky is as black as coal.

Planets are floating in a dark forest,
Waiting to be set free,
You can hear them howling miles away,
Beyond in the distance far away.

Stars are forever burning,
Like everlasting lights,
They roar in the distance,
Sparkling in the night.

Ross McKeith (11)
Doonfoot Primary School, Ayr

Why?

Why do people stare at me?
Because we look different they don't seem to see,
That underneath we are all the same,
For this trouble the whites are to blame.

But why do they treat us as if they wish we were dead?
What would happen if *we* were them instead?
I don't know why they treat us like that,
But if they were us they'd probably fight back!

So why don't we put up a fight?
Treating us like this is just not right,
But would you prefer violence and gore,
Or steadily showing them we don't like it any more?

OK, alright, but still I ask why?
Why do they think they're higher than the sky?
And that we are lower than dirt on the ground,
There still isn't any answer to be found!
The only difference between us and them,
Is because of our skin they think we're lower than them?

But blacks are black
And whites are white.
Why can't we all just get it *right!*

Shona Norval (11)
Doonfoot Primary School, Ayr

Winter - Cinquain

Winter
is coming now.
Can you spread your snow wings?
Snow angels in the snow floating.
Winter.

Lucy Clarke (10)
Drapers Mills Primary School, Margate

My Mum

My mum has . . .
A smile like a sly cat,
A laugh like a hyena,
A temper like a dog chasing a cat that can't get it,
A face like an open flower in the sun.

My mum is . . .
As mad as a gorilla,
As funny as a hyena,
As grumpy as a sad dog,
As angry as a shark that can't get its own back.

My mum has . . .
Hair like she's been pulled through a hedge backwards.
A voice like me,
A memory like an elephant,
A heart as kind as can be.

I love my mum really!

Emma-Jayne Bartin (10)
Drapers Mills Primary School, Margate

Mum!

'How long is dinner Mum, how long will it be?'
'You will have to wait a while love because
I still have to make your tea.'
'Thanks for the dinner Mum I loved the baked beans.'
'Now you can pick them off the floor on your hands and knees.'

'How long till pudding Mum, how long will it be?'
'You will have to wait a minute love because
I still have to feed your brother and me.'
'Thanks for the pudding Mum, I liked the chocolate cake.'
'That's nice to know my darling, now just give me a break!'

Kaycie Day (10)
Drapers Mills Primary School, Margate

Young Writers - Playground Poets Poems From The UK

The Box

(Based on 'Magic Box' by Kit Wright)

I will put in the box . . .

The sight of the sun setting behind
the soothing blue sea.

The salty smell of the fresh air
of the sea in the morning.

The rattling sound of a baby
gently shaking its rattle.

I will put in the box . . .

The sight of a picturesque waterfall
rolling down the steep rocks.

The smell of milky white chocolate
when I open the fridge.

The bumpy sound of a river
running through the rocks.

I will put in the box . . .

The sight of a herd of white sheep
eating the swaying grass on a summer's day.

The lovely smell of roast chicken.

The beautiful sound of a cat soothingly
purring in my ear.

I will put in the box . . .

The chocolatey smell of a chocolate covered cake.

Albina Sahiti (10)
Drapers Mills Primary School, Margate

Family

Mummy,
I love you Mum.
She loves the family,
She takes care of all of us,
She's nice.

Daddy,
I love my dad.
He is great to us kids,
He takes care of all of us lot,
He's fun.

Sisters,
They are the best,
They take you down to town,
They take you everywhere they go,
They're kind.

Brothers,
They are annoying,
They are so sweet,
They can be alright,
Football crazy.

T'Liza Powell (10)
Drapers Mills Primary School, Margate

Bulldog - Cinquain

Bulldog
The name Bulldash
Huge white teeth, big fat tum
Bulldash barking at a red cat
Bark! Bark!

Sasha Cooper (10)
Drapers Mills Primary School, Margate

My Friend Simile Poem

My friend has . . .
A smile like the shining sun,
A laugh like a chimpanzee,
A temper like a mad cow,
A face like an angel.

My friend is . . .
As mad as the Mad Hatter,
As funny as a clown,
As grumpy as a wound up bull,
As angry as a frown.

My friend has . . .
Hair like a sleek eel,
A voice like a singing bird on a sunny day,
A memory like a goldfish,
A heart as red as a rose.

Amelia Baker (10)
Drapers Mills Primary School, Margate

The Acrostic Playground Poem

P lay all day in the playground,
L ong time running around,
A stick on the floor that you found.
Y ou and me dancing around,
G oing in and out,
R ound and round.
O ut comes the rain,
U mbrellas go up and down comes the rain,
N ow it's time to go in,
D o some work and then go home!

Maddie Stanley (9)
Drapers Mills Primary School, Margate

School Dinners

School dinners are disgusting,
I had to tell you so,
I've eaten them all my life,
My mum says, 'Did you like school dinners today?'
I say, 'No, no, no!'

She says, 'It's good for you.'
But I disagree,
I say that they're horrible,
My sister thinks so too.
I just hate school dinners,
I hope you do too.

I like it when it's over,
To go back inside
And have to get some work done
With some sweeties by my side.

When the day is over,
And we all go home,
Dinners are much better
Than the ones we had at school.

Nathan Penney (10)
Drapers Mills Primary School, Margate

Parents' Evening - Cinquain

Uh-oh!
Parents' Evening
The teacher's speaking now
All the children are feeling scared
Oh dear!

Katie Cooper (10)
Drapers Mills Primary School, Margate

Don't Worry

I am very worried today,
The school bully will beat me up at play.
Mum says,
'Don't worry.'
But I am.

I am very worried this morning,
I might fall asleep in class, snoring.
Mum says,
'Don't worry,' (yawning).

I am very worried tonight,
My friend is coming over for a sleepover
And I might forget to turn off my night light.
Mum says,
'Don't worry.'
But I am.

The day went fine,
No school bully,
No snoring,
My night light was off
But there's just one little thing,
I think I'm coming down with a cough!

Ria Koster (10)
Drapers Mills Primary School, Margate

Best Friend - Cinquain

My friend,
He is so cool!
He always plays with me,
He is very good at football,
My friend.

Charlie Payne (10)
Drapers Mills Primary School, Margate

The Playground

T he school ball bounces in the air,
H e kicks it and he scores
E veryone cheers, yeah!

P ennies drop out of his pocket,
'L ook, I scored the winning goal,' he shouts,
A nd they go inside to learn.
Y achts come sailing over the puddles,
G rass is soggy, they won't be playing now,
'R ain, rain go away,' they shout,
O ut they come, it's gone now, yay, yay!
U and me can come out tomorrow,
N ow let's go home and have . . .
D inner!

Daniel Day (10)
Drapers Mills Primary School, Margate

Science - Cinquain

Science
Sometimes it's fun
But I hate it so much
It really bothers me a lot
Science.

Billie Rigden (9)
Drapers Mills Primary School, Margate

Story Map - Cinquain

'Teacher
Can you help me?
I am lost in this book.'
'Try looking at your story map.'
'It's lost.'

Sophie Crew (10)
Drapers Mills Primary School, Margate

My Football Fantasy - Cinquain

I love
playing football
at home with my new friend
and my new football and goalpost,
I score.

Scott Skinner (10)
Drapers Mills Primary School, Margate

Top Gear

My favourite programme on the telly
is one that shows cars with lots of welly,
A sports car speeding round the track,
a 4 x 4 in the dirty outback.
Yes, I would really like to appear
on a programme called Top Gear.

Several cars racing on a beach,
I wonder what speed they will reach,
famous guests in an ordinary car
on the track, how bizarre.
Yes, I would really really like to appear
on a programme called Top Gear.

Focus, Astra, Golf, Carrera
which is the hatchback of the era.
Richard, Jeremy and James present
a programme with top content!

So yes, I would really, really, really like to appear
on a programme called Top Gear!

Kyle Barnard (9)
Garden Fields JMI School, St Albans

In The Playground

I'm in the playground with my friends
playing with a ball
I'm in the playground with my friends
being careful not to fall
I'm in the playground with my friends
having a lovely time
I'm in the playground with my friends
making up this rhyme
I'm in the playground with my friends
just about to go
I'm leaving the playground with my friends
trying not to be slow.

Esther Webster (9)
Garden Fields JMI School, St Albans

My Brother Is A Demon!

My brother is a demon!
He wakes me up, he pulls my hair
He just isn't fair!
My brother is a demon!
He takes my stuff
He eats my sweets
He makes my life such a misery!
My brother is a demon!
He makes me late
He cries and cries with mischief in his eyes!
Are all our brothers demons?

Francesca Bunting (10)
Garden Fields JMI School, St Albans

Best Friends

You really need a best friend
to help you get around.
You really need a best friend
to hang around with, on the ground.

You really need a best friend
to help you understand.
You really need a best friend
to get you in a band.

So if you have a best friend
your dreams will come true,
So you don't need to worry
'cause they will always be with you.

Lucy Tinker & Alex Crowther (9)
Garden Fields JMI School, St Albans

In The Woods

I n the woods are lots of trees
N othing to stop the falling leaves.

T he birds fly through the sweetest air,
H ow graciously their great wings flair.
E verywhere is spacious and calm.

W hat is the wood's secret charm?
O ver the grass, coloured leaves lay,
O ne after the other, the wind takes them away,
D ays live on throughout the year
S ome may leave a little tear.

Phoebe Greenland (11)
Garden Fields JMI School, St Albans

Shopaholic's Daily Cycle

The addictive sea of rails await
their first swarm of victims.
They draw you in with their flowery fabrics
and sale-stamped price tags.
You pick it up just for a look,
but no, the temptation's too strong -
And then you've bought it.
Whatever it is will never last
for more than a month.
Then the next rail comes into view!

Helen King (9)
Garden Fields JMI School, St Albans

The Magic Box
(Based on 'Magic Box' by Kit Wright)

I will put in the box . . .
Me flying in a black car
My rabbit called Daisy
The flick of a cat's tail.

I will put in the box . . .
The beautiful colour lilac
Me wanting my yummy breakfast
Listing to soft music with my friends.

I will put in the box . . .
Having lots of pillow fights with my brother
Baking delicious cakes
Going to Disneyland, Paris with my friends,
Floating in the sky.

I will put in the box . . .
A puppy, smiling and
Me having the biggest ice cream in the world.

That's what I shall put in my magical box.

Alex Franklin (8)
Hammond Junior School, Lightwater

The Magic Box

(Based on 'Magic Box' by Kit Wright)

I will put in the box . . .
the wet nose of a meerkat
the white small teeth of a prairie dog
and the flat tail of a beaver.

I will put in the box . . .
the glitter from the Queen's sparkling carriage
the flag from Windsor Castle
and the swirl from the Queen's long robe.

I will put in the box . . .
the tusks of a huge pink elephant,
the sounds from the biggest, hottest volcano eruption
and the lights from the London Eye at night.

My box is made from
the softest animal skin in the world,
the box's hinges are made from a duck's beak
and its key is made from a rhino's horn.

Catherine Holmes (8)
Hammond Junior School, Lightwater

Favourite Things

(Inspired by 'Favourite Things' by Phil Bowen)

You're like the red cotton of my shirt,
You're like the blazing sun in the middle of Spain.
You're like the sweet and fizzy taste of Pepsi
On a boiling hot day.
You're like the magnificent taste of bacon and pasta
In a saucepan on a crisp winter's day.
You're like the sound of fun rock music
On a glum autumn day.
You're like the warmth of a dog's fur
On a cold winter's night.
Nobody would be better as my mum than you.

Ben Daniels (8)
Hammond Junior School, Lightwater

The Magic Box

(Based on 'Magic Box' by Kit Wright)

I will put in the box . . .
the loud roar of a lion,
a drip from the pouring rain and
the early morning glistening sun.

I will put in my box . . .
the huge tall snow-white mountains,
the sour taste of a pineapple
and the golden sky from a warm hot day.

I will put in my box . . .
the feathers of a great white swan.
The castle from far away
and the sound from a brass French horn.

I will put in the box . . .
the swirl from a queen's ballgown,
a carriage from the London Eye
and a large pink elephant.

My box is made from
10,000 light bulbs.
Its hinges are made from the Crown jewels
and its key is made from a golden carriage.

Rachel Witney (7)
Hammond Junior School, Lightwater

My Favourite Person

She has blue eyes as blue as the ocean sea,
Her fingers are as small as party sausages.
She is as bald as an old man,
She has tiny feet as small as five pencil leads.
She moves as slow as a tortoise when she crawls.
She wears bright clothes as bright as a rose.
She gurgles like a jacuzzi,
Her name is Olivia, my baby sister.

Joe Hayes (9)
Hammond Junior School, Lightwater

The Magic Box
(Based on 'Magic Box' by Kit Wright)

I will put in the box . . .
A swan floating silently on a sunray river,
A perfectly laid out sunset with golden glitter
A classical piece of music by Mozart.

I will put in the box . . .
A lavender cloud which only children can float on,
A good morning from everybody in the world and
A bark from a dog.

I will put in the box . . .
A swish of the powerful wind,
The graceful move of a dancer,
A flick of a cat's tail.

I will put in the box . . .
The huge flame of a bonfire
The swift move of a wing,
A beating heart.

My box is made of the finest gold and silver,
The hinges are made of copper
And the padlock is made of sparkling jewels.
The lid is made of stars.

Anna Kettle (7)
Hammond Junior School, Lightwater

My Favourite Person

Her eyes are like a shiny blue sky,
She is as bright as a brown owl.
Her clothes are like green leaves
Her face is like a pink rose
Her voice like a boy
She walks quietly like a lion
Her hands are brown
Her hair is as shiny as a butterfly's wings . . .

Emma Richards (9)
Hammond Junior School, Lightwater

Favourite Things
(Inspired by 'Favourite Things' by Phil Bowen)

You're like the pretty purple sky,
With jazzy music
And the fresh smell of the roast dinner,
And standing right next to my really nice friend,
And a fizzy taste of the lemonade.
And you've got a cotton jumper with a sparkling skirt with
                                stars all over,
On that boiling hot beach with a soft drink, in America.
On an exciting safari in the jungle,
On a jumping white soft horse,
The beautiful blossom floating around with pink fluffy feathers
                                coming out.
And a fresh smell of that red rose.

Eve Bushell (8)
Hammond Junior School, Lightwater

Favourite Things
(Inspired by 'Favourite Things' by Phil Bowen)

You're like the autumn leaves falling softly,
A lilac rose in full bloom,
A dolphin playing in the blue ocean.

You're like the yummiest chips I have ever eaten,
The colours of a beautiful rainbow,
A golden dress of a sparkling princess.

You're like a tulip growing in the warmth of spring,
A golden glow of the sun shining,
The fishes playing in the glittering rivers.

Eleanor Smith (8)
Hammond Junior School, Lightwater

Home From School

(Inspired by 'Childhood Tracks' by James Berry)

Eating a crispy apple,
Eating my sister's chocolate bar
Eating pasta with cheese on top
Smelling my guinea pigs eating cucumber.
Smelling my mum cooking pasta
Smelling the soap in the bathroom
Hearing the guinea pigs squeak
Hearing the floorboards creak
Hearing the wardrobe door creak
Seeing the baby robin bath
Seeing the birds nibbling the grape vines
Seeing the guinea pig gnawing the hutch.

Bradley Alma Daykin (9)
Hammond Junior School, Lightwater

Guy Fawkes' Night

Fireworks flaring in the sky with a bang,
Frightening people, marshmallows melting.
Beautiful Catherine wheels going round and round,
Ketchup squirting out of the hot dogs.
Hot mustard squirting into the burgers
Sweet toffee apples softening up by the fire
Guy Fawkes burning on the fire
Glowing sticks showing where you are.
Adults chatting, Catherine wheels twisting.
Onions sizzling in the frying pan.
Sausages falling out of the bread.
Roast pork twisting over the fire.

Sam Levey (9)
Hammond Junior School, Lightwater

Dolphins In The Sea

Seagulls squawking in the sky,
White fluffy clouds drifting by
Shiny red crabs,
Scurrying on the beach.
A boat purring as it goes by.
Fish blowing bubbles in the breeze,
Down in the stirring water caves.
Beach balls bounce and splash.

Abigail Buck (9)
Hammond Junior School, Lightwater

A Puppy In Me

I have a puppy in me
Jumping about wildly
Leaping excitedly around and around
Running about peacefully
Wanting, someone to play with
When it's bedtime, he lies down peacefully
Curling up in a ball
Making no sound at all.

Charlotte Bicknell (8)
Hammond Junior School, Lightwater

A Dog In Me

I have a dog in me
Jumping in the snow
Chasing a ball all day long
Chewing bones all the time
Chewing teddies everywhere
Trying to get puppies to play
Barking at other dogs
Wagging its tail excitedly.

Chad Goulter (8)
Hammond Junior School, Lightwater

Home From School

(Inspired by 'Childhood Tracks' by James Berry)

Eating a small bowl of rhubarb and custard,
Eating five bars of delicious chocolate.
Eating a crunchy apple.
Smelling my brother's cheesy feet,
Smelling my mum's perfume.
Smelling my yummy dinner.
Hearing my fat cat coming to me,
Hearing birds outside.
Hearing the floorboards creak,
Seeing my cats,
Seeing my mum.
Seeing the birds outside.

Christopher Nelson (8)
Hammond Junior School, Lightwater

At The Beach

The sun is shining
The water is glistening
The seagulls are flying
The children are swimming
The adults are getting a tan next to the ice cream van
The boats are fishing but the fishes aren't hungry
The dolphins are playing
The sharks are eating
The children are going for another swim in the sea
But suddenly, it's time for tea
For tea they've got a tin of tasty spaghetti
And now it's time to go home.

Lewis Paxton-Fear (9)
Hammond Junior School, Lightwater

Feelings

I am feeling as happy as a puppy,
As happy as a hyena
As bouncy as a frog
I feel swift, fast and speedy
I feel great!
I am feeling as happy as an overgrown pig
A lion, tiger, leopard and a cat,
I'm feeling good tonight.

I am feeling sad as sad can be
As sad as a snake
As sad as a flea
I am sadder than a bee
Sadder than the sea
And I am feeling sad tonight.

Ella Richardson (9)
Hammond Junior School, Lightwater

A Crocodile In Me

I have a crocodile in me
Lurking in the water
Getting ready to kill with its teeth
Moving from pond to pond
Growing and growing
Disappearing into the water
Laying over one million eggs
Lashing its tail at its prey
Killing viciously.

Oliver Cuss (9)
Hammond Junior School, Lightwater

Alley

Walking by you only see darkness,
Horrible smells and dark cloudiness
Till you walk in the scare factor comes
Teenagers smoking and getting drunk,
Graffiti covered walls and bags full of junk,
It smells of rubbish, smoke, oil and fire from the nearby kitchen
And broken down cars.
You can taste the cooking from the kitchen next door,
Moss-covered walls,
You can feel the heat under your feet,
You can see a light from the cigarettes,
It's a place to find passive smoking,
Homeless people threatening for money,
The cooks chucking out old food,
People coughing, laughing and spitting,
What a horrible place to be.
Matchsticks, bottles, rubbish and paper
All on the ground,
But now . . .
Restaurants as bright as the sun,
Shiny new stone flooring,
Full of lights bright and dim,
No left-over food
And no graffiti around,
Now it's a nice place to be.

Jasmine Gray (11)
Kingswells School, Aberdeen

The Scrapyard

The gleaming steel cars,
fresh polished paint,
Deluxe leather interior,
scents of lavender.
So many memories now faded away.
The rustic paintwork, the damp, soggy leather,
Dirt catching onto the car like a spider
catching its prey.
Tyres rotting away and scents of gloom,
Half smashed windows and doors hanging off.
Rows and rows of half destroyed cars
like a bombing had occurred.
Big machinery, hungry for destruction.
Cars pushed towards the machine,
almost screaming like they want to escape.
The machine's sharp teeth closing slowly
on the unloved car.
Closing . . . closing . . . closing
now gone . . .

Hayley Anderson (11)
Kingswells School, Aberdeen

The Park

The best condition swings,
Planks of wood as stiff as brick,
Super slidy slides as fast as a racing car,
See-saws bouncing like leaping frogs,
What a nice place the park was;
Now swings broken, swings over the top
Or covered in sticky chewing gum,
Rusty, old wood snapped, broken and all yuck,
Slides all sticky, so they are very slow,
See-saws not very bouncy, vandalised and worn out,
What an old, rusty place the park is!

Lisa Murray (12)
Kingswells School, Aberdeen

The Play Park

The stunning small slide stands
smashed and trashed,
The complex and baffling frame stands
snapped and broken.
The fresh sweet aroma tickled your nose
now overcome by the odour and stench of booze.
The elegant, mahogany bench
now a pile of snapped wood
lying on the floor.
The beautiful birds tweeting a
graceful harmony, now
decaying tin cans on the tarmac.
The velvety tulips in-between your toes,
soothe you as you graze your toes
and stand on cigarette butts.
The park is like a death zone,
The park *is* a death zone.
It is like we can't go to the park.
We *can't* go to the park.
It's like the park doesn't exist!

Sarah Milne (11)
Kingswells School, Aberdeen

Houses

Once all singing, all dancing, now boarded-up and hidden
From the fire it had dreadfully decayed.
Once it was loved with tender care, now nobody knows
There's nothing to see, there's nothing to smell
It's just your nose with lots to tell
The trees are bare, naked with no lush green leaves
They're like *zombies* lurking in the dark
These are the houses from Hell!

Robert Meiklejohn (12)
Kingswells School, Aberdeen

Football Stadium

The stadium's door creaks open with a soft sigh like an
old man out of breath,
The lime-green pitch with skilled players scoring, screamers
here and there.
The uproar of the crowd is like a terrifying dinosaur,
Players running to the crowd, celebrating the beautiful goal.
The seats are gleaming with magnificent colours
nice and shiny, in the best condition,
The heroic tunnel where the proud players came running
Out at half-time shouting, not for encouragement
but pain and warning.
We smelt smoke, the fire spread, many lives were lost,
The shrill cries of people screaming and shouting
That is the past.
The pitch has gone, mud is what is left of the once beautiful pitch,
The soft breeze whistled in my ear, nothing compared to
the loud crowd that used to be.
Nothing moved, an eerie silence filled the abandoned place
the odd insect buzzed by,
The seats were black, burnt, rusty like a player who has
just come back from an injury.
The tunnel where the fire started isn't there anymore,
vanished like a ghost.
That is now and to think what a horrible deed
I did to start the *fire.*

Mikey Christides (11)
Kingswells School, Aberdeen

The Train Station

The rundown trains
Still kept running
The broken benches
Did not budge
The vandalised walls
Were not cleaned
The sound of creaky pipes
Were not fixed
The smell of stenching fumes
Did not leave
The small abandoned ticket office
Doors were closed
The rough feel of the railings
Cut your hands
The strong smell of smoke
Made you weak
The wrecked phone box
Was a mess
This is the tortured train station
Where smokers smoke
This is the train station like a nightmare
Which dares to haunt
This is the train station just like Hell
Where nightmares are reality!

Amanda Rattray (11)
Kingswells School, Aberdeen

Boarded-Up

The boarded-up house stands tall and unhealthy,
windows smashed and wood barricading the door closed,
you can see pipes bashed in all places, holes in the roof
threatening to fall down.
The house makes you feel cold as the winter ice,
a terrible shiver crawls up your spine,
everything is quiet until you hear the sounds of loose wood
collapsing and trickles of water dripping out of the pipes.
It used to be friendly apartments, it stood so bright and healthy,
everyone was friends with everyone else but . . .
Now you can smell the paint off of the graphite wall and
horrible smoke slithering its way through the windows
from the outside world.
This isn't a place you want to visit anymore!
It's as horrible as a nightmare you can't escape from.

Leoni Forsyth (12)
Kingswells School, Aberdeen

Boarded-Up Houses

Tall and proud standing houses
with glossy peach paint.
Immense tulips stand around the garden,
singing with the sun.
But now . . .
Bricks and cement falling away at the hinges,
Mossy cars rotting away like wood.
Windows and doors swimming with nooks and crannies,
Fences rotting away with the undesirable creepy-crawlies.
Planks of wood covering the windows,
Crumbling pathways, which used to be the garden,
filled with cigarette tabs.
Slates on the roof, skimming off with the greatest of ease.
This is certainly urban decay
Worse than 1944; D-Day.

Iain McKay (12)
Kingswells School, Aberdeen

The Silent Houses

The street was so happy, the cheery laughter echoed everywhere.
But now it's like walking through the dead.
The trees used to have brightly coloured green leaves
that used to smell herby and refreshing.
But now the trees have shrunk and have gone completely naked
without any leaves.
You hear dogs panting and waiting for their owner to throw it the stick.
But now the poor dogs are tied up, crying for help,
still waiting for their owners to come.
The atmosphere was peaceful, children out playing
with a bright red ball.
But now the children never come outside to play.
It's like the wind, houses were trying to speak.
But now they've got nothing left to say.
It's like the wind was trying to say something when it growled.
But now it says nothing
But where am I?
You're in the street of silent houses.

Yasmin Livingstone (11)
Kingswells School, Aberdeen

The Park

These proud outdoor toys,
Their useful time a distant memory,
The smell of rusted metal, like a snake it suffocates,
The decaying seats once home to kind mothers and fathers,
Now is home to dead birds, caught like rats in a snare.
The rusting swings, once used by small children,
Now squeaking, twisted and snapped.
The slide once full of fun,
Now covered in a dark rainbow of dreaded spray paint.
Cracked are the steps, like a twig.
The burnt see-saw's squeak is from a rat,
The paint is flaky like dry sky.
The park is a vandal's house.

Callum Hutchinson (11)
Kingswells School, Aberdeen

Run Down Buses

The dreary outside,
The stench is Mount Everest inside.
I take one last breath
Before boarding this dreadful mess.
Teenagers smoking fags.
The seats are hedgehogs not very comfy.
I press my little face against the window
And feel a slight pain as the bits of
Glass shatter in front of me.
My eyes study the outside.
I see a vandalised shop,
An unsafe park,
A run-down pitch.
At last the bus slowly stops,
My cosy house right in front of me.
Wait!
The lock is broken
If someone had said that a year ago.
I would have just laughed.
Rewind!
The golden outside.
The sweet smell of roses, as soft as snow.
I take one last breath
Before boarding this shiny bus.
Teenagers moving to give you a seat,
The seat padding still firmly on.
I press my face against the window,
My eyes read like scanners scanning the world.
In front of me,
I see a shop full of sweets.
I see a well maintained park.
A football pitch full of fans singing their hearts out.
The bus is a cat, it cleans itself,
It slows down.
I step out and go back into my beautiful home.
Fast forward!

Jack Ironside (11)
Kingswells School, Aberdeen

The Bus Station

Cobwebs in the buses
Broken benches everywhere
Graffiti on the buses
Flat tyres
Wet paper on the roof
Pizza on the floor
Flies zooming about
Hot sick on the floor
Worms on the floor
A dead bird on the front of the station
Windows smashed
The bus is like a horrible cave
Black bats on the roof
Engine smoking
Drug dealers outside
Green moss up the walls
Black tarantula on the window.

Daniel Cowper (11)
Kingswells School, Aberdeen

The Stadium

Graffiti coated the once majestic walls
The pitch was a jungle
Silent drug dealers had replaced the roaring crowd
The statue that had once stood proud
Was now an unwashed man
The occasional gunshot could be heard
As loud as the home crowd after a goal
The smashed windows were like big black holes
Sucking in all matter it could find
A smell of urine as strong as a bodybuilder
Filled the stairwell
The walls felt slimy after years of damp
The whole stadium was silent as if trying to read the sign which said,
Demolition Scheduled For 8pm.

Daniel Busby (11)
Kingswells School, Aberdeen

The Park

Some swings are wrapped round and round, the others were
stolen or rusted,
The slide was a rocky outcrop, severely dented and covered
in a thin stream of black marker pen.
The once happy place is now left helpless and lonely.
The lush green grass is now boggy mud with glass
sticking out like thorns on a rose.
The see-saw is a gate in the night, forever creaking and screeching.
The wood supporting the structures is a heavenly haven for rot,
Time has eroded the park like rust, slowly demolishes a
strong band of iron.
The smell of half burning cigarettes is a wall surrounding the park,
keeping you out.
The benches stand empty, the climbing frame untouched,
The path overgrown,
The park forgotten.

Ben Lobban (11)
Kingswells School, Aberdeen

The Alley

The alley, so quiet and misty,
A cat creeping quietly to the overloaded bin,
Gobbling up nothing but rubbish,
Smoke gathering around a bad gang of teens,
The cat is a tiger scaring off the teenagers.
The teenagers are like deer, running from a tiger.
The alleyway is like an ugly face staring at you!
You can hear laughter from the restaurants in front,
You touch the walls, they are slimy snakes.
The stench of smoke is unbearable,
The puddles are live rivers of water everywhere.
The alley will never be the park it was before,
It will never be happy!

Victoria Moir (11)
Kingswells School, Aberdeen

Skate Park

What used to be a wonder ramp,
Now rotting away.
The metal rail
Now gone rusty,
The ramps have holes,
The grotty gate has fallen
And the vast fences are cut
And the stench of alcohol roams free.
The ramps are spider webs
And the ramp is hollow, perfect for grimy dens.
The rumbling of boarders passing for the new fancy park.
The new park is just what this used to look like,
The wacko gangsters, wrecking the park,
The ramp is rough and worn out,
It feels like the tars of a road,
The rail is like a piece of string.
The fences are like the walls of the world,
Walls that can't be seen or touched.

Drew Milne (11)
Kingswells School, Aberdeen

The Back Alley

The back alleyway is muddy and ugly;
It is as coarse as a bunch of teenagers or even as reckless.
Why couldn't it be like a beautiful butterfly, kept clean to the public?
It used to be a beautiful place with flowers and a lot of
shiny new stones.
Most people enjoyed the new back alleyway but now look at it.
It smells as bad as a farm or even dirty animals that don't get washed.
The walls are so dirty that they make you dizzy if you look at them.
You could possibly or definitely at night
See teenagers putting graffiti on the walls without a care in the world.
They would giggle and shout while they were doing it.
You might be able to touch the mud all over the wall and touch it
on your clothes.

Rachel Thompson (11)
Kingswells School, Aberdeen

The Park

The park had totally changed,
The swings were grimy with snapped chains,
The slide was colourless and covered in glass,
The climbing frame was graffiti-covered,
It was a mess!
You could smell the spray paint fumes, one sniff made you
feel weak and dizzy.
The wind blew ferociously down your neck, which made your
spine shiver.
You could hear the birds fluttering in the midnight sky,
You felt as cold as a snowman!
I wish it was back to the old times when
The park was like a funfair,
The sun was alive smiling like a happy baby,
The roundabout was a new car wheel,
spinning round like on a car.
But now it's a witch's garden.
Well at least it seems like one!

Stephi Quinn (11)
Kingswells School, Aberdeen

The Back Alley

From a car you see the back alley,
A frightening, disgusting, slimy and filthy place,
Very noisy, very creepy, very scary the alley is.
Needles on the floor along with people's clothes.
The smell of the black alley is like dog's dirt and sour strawberries.
It has wet, strong paint on the walls.
The alley is as black as a robber's clothes.
Also the path is as colourful as graffiti.

Liam Brown (11)
Kingswells School, Aberdeen

The Park

The park stood there luminous, a children magnet,
Exciting, enjoyable, it was elated, somewhere you could hang
But now the park is . . .
A sordid rundown park,
Abandoned, grotesque and revolting,
Smashed bottles lay as quiet as a mouse,
Swings had rusted away,
Drug dealers awaited for their prey,
The slide had no meaning of the world clean,
Spiders slept and mould grew,
The strong stench was disagreeable, it was ghastly,
The air felt uncomfortable, sticky as glue,
A faint sound of a creak and a owl howling like a
Washing machine in pain,
You can taste nothing, your mouth is dry!

Rachel Forsyth (11)
Kingswells School, Aberdeen

The Shop

She happily walked past it
Then started to glare
When she realised that no one was there.
The shop was abandoned with boarded up windows
And letters on the floor from the past.
The shop was in the mainstream, it used to be aesthetic,
It had fashion written all over it.
But the last few years it has changed dramatically.
The shop was dirty like a hole in the ground
And graffiti told a lot about the shop.
Unwanted clothes were left on the ground,
She smelt the revolting smell of smoke and ran away.

Lauren Cursiter (11)
Kingswells School, Aberdeen

The Back Alley

Scattered dustbins on the ground,
Smashing windows up above,
Horrible muck on the floor below,
Round the corner broken glass.
Disgusting rats, through the wall they go,
A cat runs past, hairy and wet,
Two older men come sneaking round,
A rattle came from a washing machine,
Chucked over the fence, left to die in the rain.
What happened here?
Where has this alley gone?
Where are the trees in the summertime?
Where do the children play?
What is this messy alleyway?
Where the football used to run,
Where has it gone? What happened here,
Where the children would play all day?

Catriona Webster (12)
Kingswells School, Aberdeen

Animals

A untie alligators are very angry.
N ibbling rabbits nibbling the grass.
I n their nests birds sing.
M uddy hippos are relaxing in the mud.
A giraffe can look at the world from his tall neck.
L oud lions are roaring from the trees.
S nakes are slithering through the tall grass.

Andrew Bell (10)
Marybank Primary School, Muir of Ord

The Magic Box

(Based on 'Magic Box' by Kit Wright)

I will put in my box . . .
The waves of the sea,
The call of a woodpecker hitting a tree.

I will put in my box . . .
The finest jumper from miles around,
The dust blowing through the air
And the stomp of a mad elephant.

I will put in my box . . .
A cry of a baby,
A smile of a tiger,
The first thing made in the world.

I will put in my box . . .
The first letter,
The first note,
The first TV advert.

My box is made from
Steel, rubies
And stars in the sky.

Sam Emery (8)
Minster CE Primary School, Minster

The Magic Box

(Based on 'Magic Box' by Kit Wright)

I will put in my box . . .
A magic unicorn which guards my box,
A carrot of a snowy snowman,
The first ever made teddy in the world.

I will put in my box . . .
The sharpest shark's tooth in the world,
Tinkerbell's pretty face
And a stroke of Goldilock's hair.

I will put in my box . . .
A million and one bodyguards,
A cave which guards all of my diaries
And the largest pencil case in the world.

I will put in my box . . .
A large fizzy bottle of soda,
A large portion of chips
And a mega extra cheese burger.

My box is made from
Magic horse hooves round the rim
And it works as a magnet,
It has unicorn horns for hinges
And bats in every dark corner.

I shall read my diaries
And surf up the sides and
Butterflies will lift me up to midsummer night dreams,
Never to be seen again.

Paige Allen (9)
Minster CE Primary School, Minster

The Magic Box

(Based on 'Magic Box' by Kit Wright)

I will put in the box . . .
The first time I ever made a wish,
The first picture I drew and lots of colours for my mum,
The first time I saw a friend
And looked at her like she was a beautiful girl.

I will put in the box . . .
The first tick of Big Ben,
The shiny scales off an alligator
And lots of jokes from fairies.

I will put in the box . . .
A piece of steel ice that cracks in water,
A first strand of hair from a newborn baby,
A sparkle from a fire that shines so bright.

I will put in the box . . .
The first sip of water from my bottle when I was just born,
The first cuddle from my mum,
The first smile from a brightly coloured mermaid.

My box is made from
Silver crystals and red rubies,
The hinges are like the spikes on the dinosaur's back.

I shall put in a shop that sells jewellery
And the shop is the colour of the sun
And I will go there whenever I want.

Emmylou Hamill (9)
Minster CE Primary School, Minster

The Magic Box

(Based on 'Magic Box' by Kit Wright)

I will put in the box . . .
A horn of a white unicorn,
The squiggle of a snake slipping down a slide
And a trunk of an elephant picking up peanuts.

I will put in the box . . .
A swish of a fish's tail splashing,
The wind whistling in the wind,
The click, clack of knitting grannies.

I will put in the box . . .
Ten terrifying tigers terrifying tarantulas,
The bang of a rifle shooting ducks,
The spark of an electric eel.

I will put in the box . . .
The woof of a black cat
And the purr of a white dog,
The flap of butterflies' wings.

My box is made from
Rubies, gold and ice
And babies' legs for hinges.

I shall cross the Atlantic Ocean on swift dolphins
And meet Sebastian from the little mermaid.

Oliver Coleman (8)
Minster CE Primary School, Minster

The Magic Box

(Based on 'Magic Box' by Kit Wright)

I will put in my magic box . . .
A golden harp playing softly,
An imaginary friend, Bertie the Bold,
A magic wish filled with entertainment.

I will put in my magic box . . .
A shiny shell from the seashore,
A better life for me,
A better football team for my friends.

I will put in my magic box . . .
A miaowing dog,
A barking cat,
A nicer uncle and a calmer cousin.

I will put in my magic box . . .
A day with sun and brightness,
A secret girlfriend in a West Ham kit,
A better teacher to be a bit nicer to children.

My magic box is made out of
The shiniest coin from the most fantastic tooth fairy,
A hinge made out of a burnt coin,
The most extreme coin ever.

In my box I shall
Go to a football match
And become a player for West Ham United
Football Club at Upton Park.

Daniel Adamson (9)
Minster CE Primary School, Minster

My Magic Box
(Based on 'Magic Box' by Kit Wright)

I will put in the box . . .
A swish of a horse's tail flowing in the wind,
A squeak of a mouse running across the floor,
Seven slimy snakes slithering slowly.

I will put in the box . . .
A dinosaur's bone knocking about in a basket,
A bright spark of someone cutting metal,
A rattle of pencils in a pencil case.

I will put in the box . . .
The golden hair of sweet Goldilocks,
The shimmer of a cold wind
And the flop of a letter dropping into a letter box.

I will put in the box . . .
A packet of chips being covered in vinegar,
An old book being opened
And fairy dust being dropped by Tinkerbell the fairy.

My box is made from
Shiny stones with crystals on the lid,
With rabbit ears as hinges
And love hearts in all the corners.

I shall dive with fish to the bottom of the ocean,
On the way I will meet Nemo from Finding Nemo.

Louise Cooper (9)
Minster CE Primary School, Minster

The Magic Box

(Based on 'Magic Box' by Kit Wright)

I will put in my box . . .
A last kiss from my mum and dad,
A last blink from a unicorn's eye,
A last blessing from Pope John Paul.

I will put in my box . . .
The first word from a baby's mouth,
The first cuddle I ever had,
The first person who landed on Earth.

I will put in my box . . .
The first fight the Saxons ever had,
The first sister you ever had,
The first thing ever invented.

I will put in my box . . .
The last dinosaur that lay dead,
The last alien ever seen,
The last blink before I die.

My box is made from
Hinges that are sabre tooth tiger teeth,
There will be the richest diamonds and rubies,
There will be two pieces of gold and silver
Locking it so nobody can see inside.

I shall explore the world
To discover all the history.

Sam Cornwall (9)
Minster CE Primary School, Minster

The Magic Box

(Based on 'Magic Box' by Kit Wright)

I will put in the box . . .
A silver feather of a baby sparrow,
A group of seven dwarves fat and plump
And the first smile of my sister.

I will put in the box . . .
The first tick of Big Ben,
A magic bean to see above the clouds
And a poisoned apple that is deadly dangerous.

I will put in the box . . .
The back bone of a snake,
A little rabbit that is black and white
And the first drop of water from the Atlantic Sea.

I will put in the box . . .
The gem that is sparkling red,
The first purr of a cat
And the first golden growl of a tiger.

My box is made from
Lovely rubies that are red
And shining gems on the corner,
There is silver paper on the top
And when you open the box you hear a pop.

I shall put it in the corner and see it every day
And when I get older I will give it to my grandchildren
And they can pass it on in my family.

Kieran Cowell (8)
Minster CE Primary School, Minster

The Magic Box

(Based on 'Magic Box' by Kit Wright)

I will put in the box . . .
The last kiss of a grandpa,
A magical carpet to take me anywhere
And the first smile of a newborn baby.

I will put in the box . . .
A golden wing from an ancient eagle,
The first dancing dog
And a chicken from Waterloo.

I will put in the box . . .
A white horse waving its tail into the air,
A white swan gliding through the sky
And a cushion full of feathers from all the birds in the world.

I will put in the box . . .
A shooting star from the darkest sky,
The bluest ocean in the world,
The shiniest scale from the shiniest snake.

My box is made from
Hinges that are made from the darkest tunnel full
Of secrets never to be told,
The corners are made from a mermaid's tail,
The lid is made from the finest fairy's wings in the world.

I will dance with the finest dolphins in the world
And I will surf with the sharks in the bluest sea
And I will sing with the lions.

Abigail Harrold (9)
Minster CE Primary School, Minster

The Magic Box

(Based on 'Magic Box' by Kit Wright)

I will put in my box . . .
A glint of a dragon's eye,
A swish of a dolphin's tail
And the shine of burning amber.

I will put in my box . . .
A rough scale from an ancient dragon,
The first smile of a baby
And the last Chinese whisper.

I will put in my box . . .
A tidal wave crashing over a beach of sand,
A spark from an electric eel
And the goodbye of a dead dad.

I will put in my box . . .
The first ray of a black sun,
The light of a yellow sky
And the tramp, tramp, tramp of a heavy elephant.

My box is made from
The bluest rubies and the reddest sapphires,
The hinges are golden grand gates.

I shall
Surf up the sides of my box
And land on Mars
And watch the blazing comets go by.

Brendan Durrell (9)
Minster CE Primary School, Minster

The Magic Box

(Based on 'Magic Box' by Kit Wright)

I will put in the box . . .
A glimpse of a Chinese dragon,
An ancient queen dancing
And a chicken from Waterloo clucking like it will never stop.

I will put in the box . . .
A bounce from Tigger
And a banjo from the River Nile
And a 13th month for my little brother.

I will put in the box . . .
Gates stopping the dead reaching Heaven
And daggers that are pierced by Robin Hood
And a sheep eating a wolf.

I will put in the box . . .
A shiny snake sliding down a slide
And a book that was a head
And a dog that goes *click, clack, bang.*

My box is made from
The most delicate feather in the world
And the hinges are talons of a dragon,
The corners are made from the happiness of children.

I shall play on a beach
And then dive into a sea of jelly
And jump off a cliff and on a huge trampoline.

Daniel George (9)
Minster CE Primary School, Minster

The Magic Box

(Based on 'Magic Box' by Kit Wright)

I will put in my box . . .
The first flutter of a newborn fairy's wings,
A red spotted bow from Minnie Mouse,
The leaf of a fresh tree blowing in the wind.

I will put in my box . . .
The last tick of the last hour when the sun rises,
The ring from Lord of the Rings,
The first pound out of a bank at dawn.

I will put in my box . . .
A puff of a puffy cloud up in the sky,
The magic bean from Jack and the Beanstalk trying to get away,
The whisker from a cat wiggling as fast as it can.

I will put in my box . . .
The twinkle of a star at night,
The first book ever made,
The golden egg from 'Willy Wonka and the Chocolate Factory'.

My box is fashioned with fur,
On the outside it is shaped in a heart shape,
There are gems in each corner of my box
And the hinges are like dragon's teeth.

In the middle of my box
I will have my own braiding shop every Wednesday!

Georgina Griggs (9)
Minster CE Primary School, Minster

The Magic Box

(Based on 'Magic Box' by Kit Wright)

I will put in my box . . .
The first glint of the sun on the first day of spring,
The last drop of snow on the last hour of winter,
The sound of the wave breaking onto the shore.

I will put in my box . . .
Barley sugar and people walking down a chocolate road,
Barbies that come to life with superstitious minds,
Mice wearing roller skates in a swimming pool.

I will put in my box . . .
The spoonful of sugar from 'Mary Poppins',
And the magic carpet from 'Aladdin',
The robe from the 'Goddess of the Night'.

I will put in my box . . .
A gold moon and red stars,
the number diggity doo
And a letter not imaginable.

The lid is fashioned from stars and moons
With secrets hiding in all of the cracks,
Buttons to do anything are inside the lid
And the hinges are baby dragons with emerald eyes.

I shall skim the tops of the clouds in my box
And meet angles of the sky
And see people who I thought had died.

Lauren Mackenzie-Toller (9)
Minster CE Primary School, Minster

The Magic Box

(Based on 'Magic Box' by Kit Wright)

I will put in my box . . .
The gentle flap of a butterfly's wings,
Six emerald wishes just for me,
The day I was born and the first hug I got.

I will put in my box . . .
A red moon and a white sun,
The poison from Snow White's apple,
The cackle from the wicked Witch of the West.

I will put in my box . . .
The tick-tock from a grandfather clock,
My future as a teacher in a secondary school,
A unicorn's magical horn full of all my dreams.

I will put in my box . . .
A baby zebra's first stripe,
A lion's laugh of love and a snake's shiny shimmer,
The last breath my uncle Carleton took before he died.

My box is made from
Smooth purple velvet and polished gold hinges,
With all my life secrets hiding in the corners
And a buckle on the front made of the purest brass.

I shall climb the Himalayas
And fetch a snow white unicorn at the top,
Then I shall ride down as fast as the wind can carry me on my unicorn,
All in one hour.

Laura Rochford (9)
Minster CE Primary School, Minster

My Magic Box

(Based on 'Magic Box' by Kit Wright)

I will put in my box . . .
The first football I ever got,
The baby rattle of Tigger, Pooh and Piglet.
In my box there is love from my mum and dad.

I will put in my box . . .
The first baby clothes I got,
The three wishes of my mum and dad,
The seashell that looks like the president.

I will put in my box . . .
All my baby teeth
And a mouse running away from an elephant
And an elephant with a mouse mother.

I will put in my box . . .
A silk hair in a silk sari
And a print of my birthmark
And my baby picture.

My box is made from
The finest pearl crystals in the world,
It's made from sparkling dinosaur claws
And scales of a snake.

I will help the poor in the corners of my box
And I will save them.

Christopher Smith (8)
Minster CE Primary School, Minster

The Magic Box

(Based on 'Magic Box' by Kit Wright)

I will put in the box . . .
A golden harp playing slowly,
The gleam of the sun shining
And the biggest shell in the world.

I will put in the box . . .
A bullet from the Second World War,
The first golden bird made
And the awful wish of a child.

I will put in the box . . .
The first smile of a baby,
A football in each corner
And a Chinese dragon breathing fire.

I will put in the box . . .
A shark's tooth as sharp as a razor,
A mouse chasing a cat,
Seven snakes slithering down a slide.

The hinges are made from a golden bird's wings
And the top is made from a turtle shell
And the bottom is made of an oak tree.

I shall surf the great waves of Wales
On the 5th of May 2005 in my box.

Mitchell Stokes-Carter (9)
Minster CE Primary School, Minster

The Magic Box

(Based on 'Magic Box' by Kit Wright)

I will put in my box . . .
A first cry of a newborn baby,
The last word of a grandad
And a hug from a gold dog.

I will put in my box . . .
A bag of gold and silver coins,
A cry of a crocodile crying loudly,
The first tooth of Dracula.

I will put in my box . . .
The first letter ever spoken,
A first roar of a tiger roaring away,
The hottest fire blown by a dragon.

I will put in my box . . .
The longest year in the world,
The first golden ticket for the chocolate factory
And a gold mane of a lion.

My box is made from
A gold and silver box cap.
Hinges from the fragile blaze
And corners of friendship and attraction.

I shall dig to the boundary of the world until I die
And meet the Devil or God.

Daniel Thomas (9)
Minster CE Primary School, Minster

The Magic Box

(Based on 'Magic Box' by Kit Wright)

I will put in the box . . .
The last letter in a sad book,
The first flame of a firework
And the shine of burning amber.

I will put in the box . . .
The smallest fish in the sea,
Three violet wishes from the flowers
And the last pearl of the ocean.

I will put in the box . . .
A blue bow on the sun,
A bird swimming in the sea
And a fish flying in the air.

I will put in the box . . .
The first hair of a baby lion,
A sip of the bluest water from the Indian Ocean
And a disco in the corner.

My box is fashioned from
Steel of the Iron Man for the hinges,
The top is made from a tooth from a baby
And the bottom is made from the nail of a dinosaur.

I shall build with the brownest leaves,
I shall swim like a sparkling dolphin,
I shall slide down the slidiest slide.

Andrew Waller (9)
Minster CE Primary School, Minster

The Magic Box

(Based on 'Magic Box' by Kit Wright)

I will put in the box . . .
A gold heart spreading love,
A good soul giving good in all the world
And three fairy wishes from the deepest part of fairy world.

I will put in the box . . .
The roar of a baby lion,
The last breath of a fish
And the first joke of an uncle.

I will put in the box . . .
The first cheerful smile of a baby,
Seven spiders spinning spiky webs
And a sparkle from a dragon's eye.

I will put in the box . . .
A shark with legs,
A cat that can swim
And a fish that can fly.

My box is made from shark's skin,
The hinges are made from snake heads
And the corners will be full of dreams.

I shall surf the huge seas of the world
And race boats
And I will end up on a beach the colour of Mars.

Tyler Webster (9)
Minster CE Primary School, Minster

The Magic Box

(Based on 'Magic Box' by Kit Wright)

I will put in my box . . .
A first kick of a flexible baby,
A witch on a speedy motorbike
And every colour fish in the ocean.

I will put in my box . . .
A crocodile's scaly stiff skin,
A last smile of a dolphin,
A first growl of a firm gray dinosaur.

I will put in my box . . .
The last Hallowe'en in the world,
A first tear of a lion
And six slithering snakes.

I will put in my box . . .
A horn of a bull,
A face of an elephant moving through the grass
And a big black hairy spider scattering its web.

My box is made from
Golden pearls and has sharks' teeth on the top
And spiders' fangs as the hinges.

I shall go to Australia then dance with dolphins.

Matthew Warren (9)
Minster CE Primary School, Minster

The Magic Box

(Based on 'Magic Box' by Kit Wright)

I will put in my box . . .
Five fiddlers fiddling fast,
The first cry of a baby whale,
A blue and white T-shirt from Bananas in Pyjamas.

I will put in my box . . .
The first tick of Big Ben in London,
The shoe from Cinderella and the prince,
The strike of thunder bright and loud.

I will put in my box . . .
A Roman's sword just come out of war,
A kick of a football from David Beckham,
The rose of Belle and the Beast's roar!

I will put in my box . . .
The first tooth of a baby,
A horse galloping in a hill field full of daisies,
A hug from my grandma.

The hinges are made from a £1 coin
And there is half of a sword on the lid.

I shall
Put an Irish dancing class that I go to
In it whenever I want.

Carys Wright (8)
Minster CE Primary School, Minster

The Magic Box

(Based on 'Magic Box' by Kit Wright)

I will put in my box . . .
A swish of a dolphin's tail,
A scale of a dragon
And a piece of gold crystal.

I will put in my box . . .
The golden mane of a fierce lion,
Some fire from a green dragon
And the razor-sharp teeth of a shark.

I will put in my box . . .
My old baby teeth from the past,
A Chinese tiger roaring loudly
And a white hot sun.

I will put in my box . . .
The tail fin of a fish,
The toe of an elephant's foot
And a shiny shell from the sand.

My box is made from gold, pear and crystal.
I will put in great nan and grandad.
The hinges are made of golden eagle
And the screech of a pig.

I shall skateboard inside my box
And become a professional
And do lots of tricks easily.

Carl White (8)
Minster CE Primary School, Minster

The Magic Box

(Based on 'Magic Box' by Kit Wright)

I will put in the box . . .
A baby chick of the first season hatching out of its egg,
A unicorn flying over the moon
And a twinkling star.

I will put in the box . . .
My box of dazzling crystals,
A dolphin jumping when its tail touches the seabed
And Dodger my dog.

The lid of the box is made of crystals,
The sides are made out of the bluest sapphires
And the corners are filled with diamonds with dreams inside.

In my box I shall go to Jamaica with my auntie,
We will sit on the beach eating mangoes all day.

Nishah Xeni (9)
Minster CE Primary School, Minster

Plane Kennings

A metal destroyer
A bomb carrier.

A weapon holder
A metal dropper.

A people transporter
A fast fearer.

A high-flier
A building buster.

A bomb disposer
A mechanical wonder.

I am a . . . war plane.

Daryl Ellis (10)
Miskin Primary School, Mountain Ash

Rose Kennings

A ruby centre
A time remember.

A gift giver
A pretty pitcher.

A breeze blower
An air producer.

A petal maker
A water sucker.

A bee attractor
A perfume scenter.

What am I?

I am a rose.

Sophie Lewis (9)
Miskin Primary School, Mountain Ash

Chick Kennings

An egg cracker
A soft flutter.

A yellow tweeter
A sweet singer.

A nest lover
A warm hugger.

A worm eater
A soft sleeper.

I am a . . . chick.

Jessica O'Shea (10)
Miskin Primary School, Mountain Ash

Daffodil Kennings

A garden brightener
An eye catcher.

An artist's inspirer
A spring attractor.

A national emblem
A primary colour.

An aroma scenter
A polished-like petaler.

A bee capturer
An adored flowerer.

I'm a . . . daffodil.

Kerry-Ann Clark (11)
Miskin Primary School, Mountain Ash

Sheep Kennings

A grass eater
A daisy pincher.

A coat maker
A stream drinker.

An easy scarer
A wool wearer.

A field frolicker
A mountain lover.

I am a . . . sheep.

Joshua Hall (10)
Miskin Primary School, Mountain Ash

Gavin Henson

A pride keeper
A Grandslam winner.

A great kicker
A silver booter.

A thundering tackler
An England thrasher.

A try scorer
A points creator.

A money maker
A lady-killer.

I am . . . Gavin Henson.

Courtney Brown (10)
Miskin Primary School, Mountain Ash

Foal Kennings

A newborn wobbler
A field gamboler.

A hay muncher
A stable dweller.

A super rider
A marvellous jumper.

A fence hurdler
A saddle wearer.

I am a . . . foal.

Kelsey Hall (10)
Miskin Primary School, Mountain Ash

Soldier Kennings

A gun carrier
A bullet shooter.

A flesh tearer
A bone breaker.

A mind destroyer
A life saver.

A war worker
A people attacker.

A life ruiner
A peace killer.

I am a . . . soldier.

Kelsey Lewis (10)
Miskin Primary School, Mountain Ash

Fox Kennings

A stealthy hunter
A bin ripper.

A russet wanderer
A hole dweller.

A vicious cracker
A cowardly murderer.

A blood spreader
A lamb murderer.

I am a . . . fox.

Marcus Pugh (10)
Miskin Primary School, Mountain Ash

Bomb Kennings

A shelter quaker
A metal killer.

A flesh tearer
A loud smasher.

A window cracker
A big murderer.

A people fearer
A smile taker.

A human stealer
A bone crusher.

I am a . . . bomb.

Kelsey Stevens (11)
Miskin Primary School, Mountain Ash

Blossom Kennings

A pink flowerer
A tower adorner.

A scented aroma
A petal improviser.

A seed creator
A spring beckoner.

An insect attractor
A fluttering faller.

I am . . . blossom.

Dylan Mortimer (9)
Miskin Primary School, Mountain Ash

Lily Kennings

A majestic floater
A pond adorner.

A fish hider
An insect attractor.

An artist inspirer
An eye-catcher.

A spring opener
A sunshine lover.

What am I?
I'm a water lily.

Alicia Miles (11)
Miskin Primary School, Mountain Ash

Daffodil Kennings

A spring bloomer
A yellow budder.

A beautiful aroma
A nation's emblem.

A gorgeous picturer
A motorway adorner.

A vase brightener
A stunning eye-catcher.

I am a . . . daffodil.

Rhian Lineham (10)
Miskin Primary School, Mountain Ash

Squirrel Kennings

A nut eater,
A winter hibernator.

A timid hider,
A tree climber.

A bushy-tailed creature,
A sensitive listener.

A nose twitcher,
A nest maker.

I am a . . . squirrel.

Jasmine Saunders (11)
Miskin Primary School, Mountain Ash

Rabbit Kennings

A carrot eater
A grey thumper.

A sensitive listener
A fast runner.

A high hopper
A long burrower.

A nose twitcher
A grass muncher.

What am I? A rabbit.

Jamie-Leigh Evans (11)
Miskin Primary School, Mountain Ash

Rabbit Kennings

A carrot muncher
A field hopper.

A forever dreamer
A button tail bounder.

A wonderful jumper
A harmless creature.

A sensitive listener
A smile provoker.

I am a . . . rabbit.

Laura Morgan (10)
Miskin Primary School, Mountain Ash

Daffodil Kennings

A spring bloomer
A delicate fragrancer.

A silky feeler
A national emblem.

A stunning colourer
A pollen carrier.

A sun catcher
A garden brightener.

I am a . . . daffodil.

Kelsie Neal (10)
Miskin Primary School, Mountain Ash

Kennings

A smile destroyer
A death creator.

A house bomber
A heart breaker.

A building firerer
A people upsetter.

A body skinner
A relative killer.

A city crusher
An animal howler.

I am . . . war.

Sarah O'Leary (10)
Miskin Primary School, Mountain Ash

On Top Of The Castle

On top of the castle,
There is a lovely view,
So I looked at the sky,
It was slightly blue.

On top of the castle
Where feathered birds sing,
The flowers are beautiful,
They're fit for a king.

On top of the castle
The sea waits below,
Colours of blue and green
As the moon reveals its glow.

Bradley Mullen (10)
Mornington Primary School, Nottingham

My Bedroom

I walk in my bedroom and what do I see?
I see there is everything all for me.
When I'm angry, when I want to kill
It's a place for me to chill.

When I'm annoyed and going to sink
My bedroom is a place to think.
When there is no one here with me
It is a place to be.

A bedroom is a place to chill
Whether I'm feeling well or ill.
Me and my friends hang out in there,
My room has got its own flair.

Whenever I need a place to be
My bedroom is special to me.

Charlie Bexon (10)
Mornington Primary School, Nottingham

Standing Here Upon The Deck

Standing here upon the deck
I cast my eyes across the sea,
Wind blowing through my hair.

Standing here upon the deck
Glittering fish dive through the waves,
Wiggling, jumping high in the air.

Standing here upon the deck
I see an island view not far away,
I cast my eyes to the shore,
I spy a peaceful beach not far away.

Joshua Moumchi (10)
Mornington Primary School, Nottingham

My Special Place - Bulgaria

The snow glistening in the sun,
The skis slicing through the carpet of snow,
The mountains overlooking the beautiful landscape,
This is why Bulgaria is special to me!

The sky is smiling and laughing,
Everyone falling and flying,
People screaming and shouting,
This is why Bulgaria is special to me!

The snow is falling through the air,
The snow sticking to people's hair,
The clouds shine in the light,
This is why Bulgaria is special to me!

The Frenchmen screaming,
The Englishmen laughing,
The Italians crying,
This is why Bulgaria is special to me!

The lights shining at night,
The music playing from the bars,
People getting drunk over their cocktails,
This is why Bulgaria is special to me!

Jamie Ball (10)
Mornington Primary School, Nottingham

This Is Our Home

Our home isn't a house of clay,
Our home is a place where we all stay.
Not a hotel, not a flat,
Our home is Earth, as simple as that.
This is our home.
Round like a ball, blue like the sea,
Green like the grass, home for you and me.
A place of reason, a place of friends,
We'll all live here until it ends.
This is our home.

Connor Chettle (11)
Mornington Primary School, Nottingham

Funfair

It was cold and wet
At the wonderful Goose Fair,
Everybody was having fun
With a lot of time to spare.

Funfair, funfair,
Lots of fun and time to spare.
Funfair, funfair,
The weather is poor but we don't care.

All the rides are fun and scary,
Brill and fab all over the place.
The children say, 'Can we go on that again?'
With a massive pleading smile on their face.

Funfair, funfair,
Lots of fun and time to spare.
Funfair, funfair,
The weather is poor but we don't care.

All you can hear is shouting and screaming,
It smells like burgers and chips,
Seeing all of the people there
And watching the clowns do their flips.

Funfair, funfair,
Lots of fun and time to spare.
Funfair, funfair,
The weather is poor but we don't care.

The funfair was excellent,
But sadly it is about to end.
We will come back next year
With a bit more money to spend.

Funfair, funfair,
We will be back next year.

Jonathan Huggard (11)
Mornington Primary School, Nottingham

My Mountain Of Dreams

Inside my mountain of dreams,
Wherever I go it seems,
I dream I'm skiing on pure white sugar
And falling down on hard, flat rubber
Inside my mountain of dreams.

Inside my mountain of dreams,
Wherever I go it seems,
Fantastic views
Of mountains in queues,
Inside my mountain of dreams.

Inside my mountain of dreams,
Wherever I go it seems,
I'm drifting away,
But that is OK,
Because I have a mountain of dreams.

Victoria Thorpe (11)
Mornington Primary School, Nottingham

The Countryside

A place where I can sit and dream
As the peaceful wind blows through
My long, curly brown hair.

A place where rabbits jump
Through the tall blonde wheat,
Where the bright summer sun
Shines through as the day breaks.

A place where birds fly overhead
With their wings flapping calmly in the breeze.

A place where horses walk on the muddy, hard ground,
Their horse shoes clomp fast in a rhythm.

A place where butterflies sweetly float
In the calming breeze.

Rebecca Armstrong (11)
Mornington Primary School, Nottingham

Who Am I?

In my bedroom
I see the carpet as candyfloss floating,
The ceiling as the beautiful clouds swaying,
The bed is just about to sail away.

The telly as the treasure box saving up the good,
The PS2 as the animal box with a fox to eat inside,
My lamp as my secret spy system watching out for the bad.

The light from the lamp shining tells me that we are near shore,
We go to raid the land but we found nothing,
We sail away to find another land . . .
But all we found was sand.

Night-time is near, we eat our meal and go to sleep
But I peer to see if we're near land!

Who am I?

Sabrina Akhtar (10)
Mornington Primary School, Nottingham

My Special Place In Spain

The calm sea glistening in the sunlight,
Golden grained sand lying on the ground,
The beautiful landscape
And that's why Spain is special to me.

The noisy bars in the town,
Heat blowing towards me,
The lovely tasting cocktails
And that's why Spain is special to me.

The heat of the outdoor swimming pool,
Waves lashing in the deep blue ocean,
The scorching heat
And that's why Spain is special to me.

Andrew Jobe (10)
Mornington Primary School, Nottingham

Under The Sea

U nder the sea the creatures play,
N ext to the rock the crabs peck,
D own below the dolphins work,
E ager to find food the shark surrounds,
R acing through the bay the sea horses cheer.

T he seagulls sit on the water to collect food,
H igh above the sea snakes tangle,
E els sliver through the waves.

S eeking through the water the sun reflects,
E ating fish the shark hunt their prey,
A beautiful crystal-blue whale enters the sea.

Lauren Palin (10)
Mornington Primary School, Nottingham

Beach

Just imagine . . .

B right, shiny glitter reflecting back,
E legant, calm palm trees sway,
A larm warning as the sea comes closer,
C hill as the waves gently lap at your feet,
H oliday people touring the island.

Sophie Cook (10)
Mornington Primary School, Nottingham

Beach

B eautiful bright coloured baby-blue beach,
E gyptian glitter gold shining at us,
A ncient fossils in the seas.
C rabs snapping at your feet,
H ollow, hard rocks at the bottom of *clear water*.

Hollie Raven (11)
Mornington Primary School, Nottingham

The Beach

T he beach is peaceful, quiet and calm,
H e holds soft golden sand in his palm,
E normous waves crash upon the shore.

B eautiful sunrays, we want some more,
E ach palm tree waves a green leaf,
A t midday the sun is a shadow thief,
C old breeze as the sun disappears,
H ome time is near, as the stars appear.

Elly Passingham (10)
Mornington Primary School, Nottingham

The Field

T he field is so green, calm and quiet.
H unting foxes creeping through the tall, thin grass
E ating rabbits like they've never eaten before.

F lowers are so bright, yellow and blue,
I nsects are hopping to and fro.
E verything is peaceful and green,
L eaves are scattered brown and quiet,
D aylight is so bright all day through.

Charlotte Shelbourn (11)
Mornington Primary School, Nottingham

Lady Of The Ocean

T he tide creeps in, enveloping the golden sand,
H er blue satin coat whispering to the land,
E ast of the beach wind floats by

B ashing the rocks, boasting to the sky,
E bony doesn't appear over here,
A wesome view, glistening clear,
C astles of sand, disappear away,
H ere lies the end of our beautiful day.

Lauren Turner (11)
Mornington Primary School, Nottingham

Dreaming Of Heaven

I would do anything or everything to reach Heaven
But all you really have to do is count to eleven.
There is a place on our planet
Where you will find your dreams' desire,
Humungous glistening mountains spread in a white butter,
The view stabs your naked eye with its blinding prettiness.
You hear the gentle squeak of the macaw penguin
Signalling a peaceful message to a ducking walrus.
An uninhabited chalet village
Awaits your arrival with an eternal flame,
Trees sway in the warm breeze
As you get down on your knees and pray to the god of happiness
That this great sensation will last for ever.
All great things have to come to a dramatic end
As it fades away, with the beginning of a new day.

Aidan Southall (11)
Mornington Primary School, Nottingham

Unicorn Beach

When I open my eyes I see . . .
A beautiful golden beach
Where the sea is rolling calmly like a galloping horse,
Where the sand is so hot you can't take off your shoes,
Where the sky is just as blue as the sea
And the sun is giving everybody beautifully brown bodies,
Where there are unicorns acting like donkeys,
Giving people rides up and down the beach,
Where everybody is having the best time of their lives,
But when I open my eyes I see . . .
My world, a world that makes me feel disappointed.

Ellie Richmond (10)
Mornington Primary School, Nottingham

Skiing

The white cool snow asleep,
The mountains way up high start to look steep.
The chair lifts like to gaze down while they stop,
When we move it's time to pop off.
Those gondolas go fast so get in those boots and skis,
On the black line
I don't feel fine,
Coming down snow spits in my face
But it is a very strange place.
The snow drifting off the ground,
I think the snow is hearing sounds.
I get off the gondolas at the top in the slushy ice,
I look up to the top of the sky,
The clouds are floating down by
Emptiness but they try not to die.

Lucy Stirland (10)
Mornington Primary School, Nottingham

Hell

In Hell it never rains,
Rage is amongst the ghastly beings.

The red-hot fire burns like a hot oven,
Melting all in its path of destruction.

As Satan cackles you sense the evil and rage.

Hell is a place where there is no rules,
Only anger and pain.

Hell is a place where murderers roam,
Their fear in their eyes is enough to kill a bird.

Jordan Towers (11)
Mornington Primary School, Nottingham

Earth From Space

I gazed down and saw . . .
Great white clouds dancing lazily,
Turquoise-blue sea splashing, spraying,
Gentle islands swaying in the breeze,
Massive cliffs loom over the shore,
Hilly fields peacefully lying,
Tall snow-topped mountains pierce the clouds,
Passing over a rainforest at dawn,
A huge rapid river makes its journey to sea,
Pyramids stand old and crumbing,
Asian cities, buildings beyond belief,
Supertankers scar the Indian Ocean,
Uluru stands proud, landmark of the desert,
Weightlessly I floated around the Earth,
Seeing sights only few men have seen!

Christopher Churchman (11)
Mornington Primary School, Nottingham

My Dream Place

My land of chocolate milkshake and more,
Through the earth and to the core.

When it rains coffee falls,
There is chocolate melting in the malls.

I look from a cloud
And I feel very proud.

Hills of massive Maltesers ten times
Bigger than a crowd of golden retrievers.

When it snows, it snows white Maltesers,
It piles up higher than white retrievers.

Jack Barnes (11)
Mornington Primary School, Nottingham

My Bed

My bed was a ship on top of the sea,
The covers were rolling, gently rocking me.
The mattress was bouncing, waves crashing on the shore,
Mum's icy hand shakes me and I see it no more.

My bed was a tree in the African suburbs,
Calm village locals make ointments with herbs.
Playful lion cubs roll around in the grass,
It vanishes as my brother shrieks, 'You'll be late for class!'

My bed was a dog basket, warmed by the fire,
Flickering flames grow higher and higher.
A gentle pat as I gnaw on my bone,
It's gone as Dad calls, 'You're needed on the phone.'

My bed is a limo carrying me to fame,
Up on stage I sing my song again.
I catch roses from my adoring fans,
Our cleaner wakes me up, clattering pans.

My bed is heaven, a comforting hug,
It's like sipping from a hot chocolate-filled mug,
It's warm and cosy, quiet and cool,
It's a shame I have to go to school!

Emmeline Wilcock (10)
Mornington Primary School, Nottingham

My Dream

A room full of icing that you can ski down,
A swimming pool of lemonade please, do not frown,
With chocolate square walls
And big Malteser balls,
A big stereo to make a big sound.

I have a big football pitch,
It makes me look rich
And that is all of my dream.

Tom Guile (11)
Mornington Primary School, Nottingham

My Chocolate Mountain

I'm standing on top of my chocolate mountain
Looking at the beautiful view!
I'm standing on top of my chocolate mountain
Eating my way through!
I'm standing on top of my chocolate mountain
Listening to the peaceful sound!
I'm standing on top of my chocolate mountain
And then some sweets I found!
I'm standing on top of my chocolate mountain
High up in the sky!
I'm standing on top of my chocolate mountain
Watching the birds fly!
I'm standing on top of my chocolate mountain
Then I stepped on a candyfloss cloud!
I'm standing on top of my chocolate mountain
All of a sudden it went loud!
I'm standing on top of my chocolate mountain
Oh, what a great dream this has been!

Tina Bozorgi (10)
Mornington Primary School, Nottingham

Antarctica

A place where the ice glistens in front of the sunburnt sky.
Narrow ice cliffs fall peacefully into the calm and gentle sea.
To the surprise of the penguins the polar bears sleep on the
icebergs that float out to sea.
A cold rustling wind sprints across the icy beach making the sea fresh.
Rain crystals hang calmly from the ice tunnels.
Circular rainbows dangle from the sky catching attention from below.
Tickling raindrops settle in the pure white snow.
Icebergs melt to form a new sea to start their new adventure.
Crispy snow hardens during the moonlit sky.
A pleasant setting calmly fades away.

Daniel Turner (11)
Mornington Primary School, Nottingham

Heaven

Heaven is where I long to be,
Where with my own eyes I would see . . .

Swirling clouds so far below,
Yet space will never be higher than Heaven,
With its golden gates shining ever, ever so bright,
Searing through the night
With its awesome light.

I'd open the gates of Heaven
And take a shy step into the world beyond,
Where I would be greeted by old friends
And choirs of angels singing God's song.

This is where I long to be,
Sitting with God, Christ and all the angels.

Sam Boneham (11)
Mornington Primary School, Nottingham

As I Stand Here

As I stand here and look out across the sea
I can feel the golden sands between my toes,
The warm breeze blowing across my nose.

As I stand here and look out across the sea
I can hear the seagulls scavenging for food,
Scavenging and flapping, trying to feed their brood.

As I stand here and look out across the sand
I can see the donkey walking round and round,
Chasing waves up and down.

As I stand here and look out across the sand,
Children playing, laughing, shouting,
Ice cream melting in the scorching sun.

Glen Daley (11)
Mornington Primary School, Nottingham

The Land In My Dreams

There is a land in my dreams
Where I can escape
From reality that seems
To wrap around me like tape.

Unicorns gracefully glide by
Striding elegantly across the land
Tropical birds taking over the sky
The sun beating out its popular demand.

Waterfalls glisten pearly-white
Cascading gently onto the rocks below
Catching the ever shining light
The sun giving off an earthly glow.

Mischievous pixies dancing around
Playing tricks on whoever they can find
Shy horseflies not making a sound
All this is going on inside my mind.

My special land
My special world
My special dreams . . .

Serena Kaur Johal (11)
Mornington Primary School, Nottingham

World In My Dreams

Thick blankets of snow,
That no one else will ever know,
Because this world is in my mind,
That no one else will ever find.
My world comes true in my dreams,
The moon shines down and the snow gleams,
As I wander through my land,
I pick some snow up with my hand,
The snow will melt and it has gone,
My dream went with it but not for long.

Natasha Heaps (10)
Mornington Primary School, Nottingham

Animals Everywhere

A nimals are everywhere
N early always here and there
I guanas are mostly up trees
M onkeys have hairy hands and knees
A nimals are insects too
L ions are bigger than you
S nakes are long like a baguette.

E lephants never forget
V ipers spit out poison
E verybody's killing animals
R eptiles are like cannibals
Y o-yos act like kangaroos
W hen they hop out of the blue
H ippos swim in the river
E agles make me shiver
R abbits with their tails of fluff
E mus strutting out their stuff.

Tevin Sahota (10)
Mornington Primary School, Nottingham

Chocolate World

Chocolate stays as the sun begins to rise,
After the heat the chocolate dies,
The chocolate river is so smooth,
The river boiling so I groove,
The chocolate is so very fine,
It might even be divine,
This chocolate world,
Is very, very bold,
These chocolate houses are so sweet,
You can't even feel the beat,
Chocolate people dance around,
They have a cheerful sound,
When I open my eyes,
I am not surprised.

Ajay Sohal (11)
Mornington Primary School, Nottingham

Heaven

When I lie down on my bed,
I snuggle up to my warm ted,
I fall asleep so I can dream,
About the sky, the light, the beam.
My imagination flows,
I feel a trickle through my toes,
I skip into my dreams of Heaven,
Sky is dreamy, scenes of Devon,
Clouds are waving in the air,
I step on gently taking care,
Kids are screaming on the rides,
Parents watching on the sides,
Children licking fudge ice cream,
Reps on stage with the kids' team,
They are dancing having fun,
Eating chocolate, having buns,
I am standing on the sea,
All the people look at me,
I feel warm down deep inside,
But I am frightened by the tide,
People tell me it's OK,
By how calm it is when children play,
Nothing harms me since the tide,
Heaven is long and Heaven is wide,
I travel the skies flying right by,
Kicking my legs, saying goodbye,
I wave at my dream, leaving Heaven to rest,
Hoping for it to stay at the best.
It was all my calm temptation . . .
But really it was an imagination.

Sophie Avci (11)
Mornington Primary School, Nottingham

Place Up There . . .

There's a place up there for me and you,
Where all our dreams shall soon come true.
All the spacecraft fly to the cream cheese moon,
The dolphins dive in a cool lagoon.
The candyfloss glides in the soft pink dawn,
The owls coo safely in the calm, fresh morn.
The waterfall flows below the glowing sun,
Sunbathing mums, dads having fun.
Diving in the sea with tropical fish,
Our parents grant our every wish.
I can smell the toffee apples, hear the screams,
People on rides, fulfilling their dreams.
The fairground music comes my way,
But I can't waste another day.
I escape to exactly where I need,
A place of no hunger, only greed.
Candy cane trees lay on the floor,
All the locals can scoff no more.
Why has this heaven been destroyed?
It leaves me angry and annoyed.
There are people in the world out there,
Who, about the environment, do not care.
For if you dream way too hard,
From this fantasy you'll be barred,
But if you think at the correct pace,
The dream will be lived, it'll be your place.
If this tranquillity's your temptation
Just close your eyes, use your . . . imagination.

Mollie Carberry (10)
Mornington Primary School, Nottingham

My Imagination . . . Underwater

In my imagination I see . . .
A gold goldfish as true as can be
Turtles surround me 10 centimetres tall
And as I speak they hear my call
Clownfish live in the anemones
To keep out their vicious enemies
Dolphins jumps have no end
Dolphins fly and gracefully bend
The seaweed slithers around the sand
And then gets attached to my hand
Sharks eat everything
They are oceans' king

My imagination is my own
To no one else it can be shown.

Reena Dewshi (11)
Mornington Primary School, Nottingham

The Doorway

My doorway to dreams
Is not far away
It's Heaven it seems
That's what I say
When walking through
I feel my flight
It's not a lie, I know it's true
I fly up like a joyful kite
Diving into the sparkling sea
The sea is bright like the sky
Here your hopes will be set free
In this great place you will never die.

Daniel Pacey (11)
Mornington Primary School, Nottingham

The Island

My favourite place is the best place ever
It always has the most fab weather!
Clear blue water, soft white sand, the warm, gentle wind passes
my hand.
Pineapple juice in a coconut cup
In two minutes I have drunk it all up.

Mothers, fathers, girls and boys
In the gorgeous sea with their rubber toys.
I wish I could stay here forever and ever
This endless daydream is the best
It is so much better than the rest.

This heavenly island remains nameless
Now that this daydream is over and done with
I will be on this island very soon.

Yasmine Zeidan (11)
Mornington Primary School, Nottingham

Atmosphere Of The Beach

The glistening crystal sea sparkled
As the warm welcoming wind blew across my face
Sapphire-blue clouds spoke to me from far above in space
The golden bronze sand stretches across for miles
Tall, swaying palm trees give me shelter
The razor-hot sun tries to get to my skin
The strong smell of seaweed I soon get used to
The flowing song of the sea goes peacefully through my ears
I rest calmly as the sun goes down.

Aneesa Khan (11)
Mornington Primary School, Nottingham

The Beach

The calm sea slowly creeps up onto the golden sand,
I can see the seagulls peacefully gliding around in the clear blue sky,
As the wind blows by, I hear it whisper, 'You are not alone.'
The water in the rock pools ripple as the sea creatures have an
afternoon swim,
When I quietly tiptoe across the beach, the sand calmly tickles my feet,
The beach is my favourite place, full of secrets and surprises.

Amy Ellison (10)
Mornington Primary School, Nottingham

War Of The Weather

Smell of sulphur hanging in the air
Menacing black clouds haunting the sky
Dogs getting restless pacing up and down
Treetops raging in the wind trying to escape the icy blast
Flashing lightning ripping through the sky
Sending static up your spine
Thunder drumming like raging soldiers marching to war
The war has begun
Rain crashing at rooftops
Wind raging at the trees
Pulling them from the ground
Lightning torching the sky
Torturing the ground
Thunder roaring, commanding the storm onwards into battle
The storm is gone
The battle won
A distant dog baying in reply to the howling wind
Clouds parting
Trees straightening
Light returning.

Cameron Souter (10)
New Gilston Primary School, Leven

The Three Little Pigs

Mummy pig said to her babies one day,
'The time has come for you to go on your way.'
The first little pig made his house of straw,
The wolf's mouth was watering at what he saw,
The big bad wolf shouted, 'Let me in!'
'Not by the hairs on my chinny, chin, chin.'
'Then I'll huff and I'll puff and I'll blow your house in.'
He ate the pig and he howled and he cried,
'My stomach still is not satisfied!'
He went to the house of sticks,
The wolf was already licking his lips,
The wolf shouted, 'Let me in!'
'Not by the hairs on my chinny, chin, chin.'
'Then I'll huff and I'll puff and I'll blow your house in!'
He ate the pig but he howled and he cried,
'My stomach still is not satisfied!'
The next house was not of straw, not of sticks,
This clever pig made his house of bricks.
The wolf shouted, 'Let me in!'
'Not by the hairs on my chinny, chin, chin.'
'Then I'll huff and I'll puff and I'll blow your house in!'
The wolf blew, blew, blew and blew,
But the house stayed up as good as new,
So the wolf jumped down the chimney after his desire,
But he did not see the deadly fire!
As the wolf was gone the house was full of laughter,
Then the third and final pig lived happily ever after!

Simon Scott (11)
New Gilston Primary School, Leven

Ten Purple Penguins

Ten purple penguins trying not to whine
One couldn't do it, then there were nine.

Nine purple penguins trying to squash in a crate
One didn't fit in, then there were eight.

Eight purple penguins, one of whom was Kevin
He fell and bumped his head, then there were seven.

Seven purple penguins putting on lipstick
One looked horrible, then there were six.

Six purple penguins learning how to drive
One crashed the bus, then there were five.

Five purple penguins doing all their chores
One had asthma, then there were four.

Four purple penguins having afternoon tea
One had a headache, so then there were three.

Three purple penguins meeting Winnie the Pooh
One got stuck in honey, then there were two.

Two purple penguins eating a sticky bun
One got its beak stuck, then there was one.

One purple penguin dressed up as a nun
He tripped on the robe, then there were none!

Kirsty Souter (8)
New Gilston Primary School, Leven

The Storm

Heavy black clouds,
Lumbering across the sky,
Wind howling in your ear,
Like a hungry wolf,
Flashing lightning,
Cutting through the sky.

Raindrops battering the windows,
Thunder rumbling like a distant drum,
Stinging raindrops hitting like sharp daggers,
Thick smell of thunder hanging in the air.

Light appeared in a flash
Searing through the black sky,
Lighting up the Earth for a split second.

Hailstones hurling like tiny silver comets,
Rumble of thunder,
Sounding again, nearer now.

Wind grabbing at the trees,
Pulling them to the ground,
Blinding light once more,
Illuminating the scene around.

Thunder due any moment . . .
Boom!

Corinne Orr (10)
New Gilston Primary School, Leven

School Day

Mum screaming
Children sleeping
Mum shouting
Clocks ringing
Teeth brushing
Breakfast eating
Uniform dressing
Hair combing
Jake yapping
Door opening
Children running
Bell ringing
Everybody working
At school.

Katie Lamb (8)
New Gilston Primary School, Leven

Going to School

Door closing
Sun shining
Stones crunching
Cars rushing
Everyone walking
People running
Everyone shouting
Everybody playing
People moaning
Bell ringing
Everyone stamping.

Bryce McLaughlin (8)
New Gilston Primary School, Leven

Going On Holiday

People packing
Mums shouting
Children screaming
Dads relaxing
Babies crying
Case packing
Car filling
Bags squishing
Everyone sitting
Dad driving
Music blaring
Car stopping
Excitement building
Doors opening
At hotel arriving
Children sleeping
Dad snoring
Mum snoozing
Dawn breaking
Everybody awaking
Family changing
Sunbathing
Pool swimming
Shops visiting
Bargain hunting
Money spending
Souvenir buying
Barbecues burning
Food chomping
Everyone relaxing - holiday.

Ashleigh Wallace (10)
New Gilston Primary School, Leven

Hide-And-Seek

Game starting
People joining
Sentences picking
People fussing
Eyes closing
Tigger counting
People choosing
Some running
Everyone hiding
Eyes opening
Tigger searching
Nothing moving
Tigger spotting
People revealing
Tigger tiptoeing
People helping
Help searching
People finding
Extra revealing
Little cheating
Few hiding
Hard finding
Tigger stopping
Two winning
Game stopping
Fun hiding.

Jacob Lamb (9)
New Gilston Primary School, Leven

Coming Home From School

Bell ringing
Children barging
People running
Cars whooshing
Rain pouring
Lights flashing
Birds twittering
Trees swishing
Grace chattering
Eleanor singing
Doors slamming
I'm home.

Duncan Sinclair (9)
New Gilston Primary School, Leven

Sword Swallower By Henri Matisse

(Inspired by the painting)

In the picture I can see:
A man standing bold and brave
With a face as pale as winter.
Eyes jet-black as a dark night
Teeth like metal bolts
He has been struck by swords.
Swords emerge from his mouth:
Pain and fury, blood and gore.

Blinded by the brightness of the colours,
Slowly and silently,
He falls to the floor.

Alex Roby (11)
Nicol Mere Primary School, Wigan

Weeping Woman

Hair of many colours,
Praying for hope,
Weeping with sorrow for her injured child,
Blinded by her tears,
White with fear,
Eyes wet with tears of love
Scared for her dying child,
Heart pounding,
Silence.
Only dripping of tears can be heard
Drip-drop, drip-drop
Slowly hitting the ground.
She sits alone,
Could this be the end?

She fears the worst, the worst has come,
The little child lies on the floor,
Cold, resting in peace.
Mourning the death of her beloved child,
The sorrowful mother weeps in despair,
Eager to believe that her child still lives,
The mother can still hear the heartbeat of the youth.

She is dying of heartache,
Her broken heart turns cold, cold and black,
Ever so slowly, the mother dies.

Pebbles Kay-Traynor (11)
Nicol Mere Primary School, Wigan

In The Picture

In the picture I can see,
A sparkling star smiling at me.
Its arm shivered in the night sky,
Its stardust fell to the ground.
The starlight reflection was in the lake,
The water ripples were shivering.

Caitlin McAleavy (8)
Nicol Mere Primary School, Wigan

Belshazzar Sees The Writing On The Wall

(Inspired by the painting)

There is a banquet
In the presence of Belshazzar,
There is smoke for seconds,
Then all becomes clear.
Belshazzar and guests see the writing,
Being written by a lone hand.
The writing glows a threatening glow.
The glow of the writing blocks out all other light,
Everyone petrified except one woman in purple.
The woman in red cowering before the glow of writing,
Spilling wine as she falls.
In the shadows of the room the outline of a child,
The child playing her silent flute,
A ghost maybe?

The writing is a threat:
Belshazzar had better change.
What will happen to him and his guests?
Will Belshazzar lose all his wealth?
Present happenings cause the woman in black to faint.
Will anyone survive?
Only time will tell.

Michael Lavelle (11)
Nicol Mere Primary School, Wigan

In The Picture

When I look in the picture,
I see a scarlet sky
And the sun setting
Ready to create darkness.
The swimming pool turns yellow,
With the reflection of the moon.
The people gather round,
Wearing ponchos
To dance the night away.

Emily Appleton (7)
Nicol Mere Primary School, Wigan

The Fight By L S Lowry

(Inspired by the painting)

A dark and dusty road,
Outside a shabby old boarding house.
As innocent passers-by witness a fight of passion,
Two proud men in love with one woman.
The shock of the first punch strikes the bystanders,
As dogs mooch loose from their owners' leads.
They watch a scuffle for honour,
The anger rages as punches and kicks are thrown.
They fall weaker and weaker as the day grows old,
More crowds gather as shouts turn to chants.
Who will triumph? No one knows.
They suddenly stop and turn away,
This fight will end with no victor
Both men turn toward their shelter.

Ryan West (11)
Nicol Mere Primary School, Wigan

In The Picture

In the picture I can see,
A bat in the spooky, dark bat house
I can see a monkey in a tree
I see a lion dozing under the tree
I see a barn owl gazing at me
I see an elephant wondering
I see a bear wandering around
I see a zebra running around
I see a giraffe eating some leaves on the tree
I see three monkeys fighting over a baby monkey.

Chloe Sherman (7)
Nicol Mere Primary School, Wigan

Le Train Dans La Neige By Claud Monet

(Inspired by the painting)

The train's lights beaming straight in front.
Standing hard on the rails.
It seems 100 miles long and more.
Big, loud noises as they pass.
Steam blowing every way.
People's eyes clogged up with soot.
Scarlet skies turn to grey.
The day blackens into night
And the air's polluted up with smells.

Snowflakes gently touch the ground.
Trees and gates topped with snow.
The snow is wet.
Are you cold?
Everybody wishes they were home.
Old grey trees tower to the skies.
Tall grey buildings still as a statue.
Lamps lit next to the tree.
People wrapped up warm.

Impatient crowds waiting to board.
Sighs and cries of boredom.
Children clinging to their parents so they don't get lost.
Different heads bob up and down.
Then the driver shouts, 'Jump aboard.'
Celebrations of joy.

Melanie Edwards (10)
Nicol Mere Primary School, Wigan

Poppy Field At Argenteuil

(Inspired by the painting by Monet)

A sea of red,
A carpet of green grass,
Trees swaying in the wind,
Beautiful daffodils in the background.
The blue sky a carpet of silk,
A scintillating view from the house.
Streams of long poppies,
Shaded blue sky,
A stream of people striding through the poppies,
Shaped clouds in the sky.
No one notices the green trees in the far meadow,
Because of the red beauty.
The house in the distance old and empty,
No one to be seen.

Christopher Pope (10)
Nicol Mere Primary School, Wigan

Little Dancer Aged 14

(Inspired by a painting)

She stands tall and proud with her head up high,
Her jaw like an animal muzzle,
Her flowing hair tied up tight.
A smile starts to appear through her lovely, calm face.
Her shoulders rest with happiness as her feet go into fourth position,
Poised, one at the front and one at the back.

The ribbons flare out,
The dress flowing as she dances her graceful ballet dance.
Her short muslin skirt rests as the end appears.
That young Egyptian girl, age 14.

Alysha Whittle (11)
Nicol Mere Primary School, Wigan

The Night Watch By Rembrandt

(Inspired by the painting)

The guns are loaded
Their eyes are peeled
The hounds are raring
The pikes are pitched
The child is retreating
The drummers drumming
Armour is at the ready
Tactics have been discussed
Midnight strikes
Swords sharp
Nerves jingling
Eyes bulging
Heads turning
Armour shiny
Reserves waiting
Feet tapping
Swords ready
Mouths opening
Pockets overflowing with ammunition
They are ready for battle, so beware!

Sam Spruce (11)
Nicol Mere Primary School, Wigan

In The Picture

In the picture I can see,
Wonderful, high, green mountains disappearing into the clouds
In the picture I can see,
High roads looking down into the green hills and white, curly sheep.
In the picture I can see,
Farmers in their big tractors mowing the big, thick, fresh grass.
The animals making funny noises!
In the picture I can see,
My family enjoying a long walk.

Lydia Wadsworth (8)
Nicol Mere Primary School, Wigan

The Graukler Family
(Inspired by the painting by Picasso)

They used to work at the circus
But walked out of the doors
And never returned.
Now lost and not found,
They grow exhausted and famished
But wearily conquer the dusty desert road,
And the distant darkening sky seems to devour the rocky hill path.
They scavenge for rations
But find no food.
They search for water
But find no spring.
And the daughter in the wild land
Squeezes her father's wrinkly hand.
The jesters and the acrobats
Weep and whine all through the night.

Richard Draper (10)
Nicol Mere Primary School, Wigan

Icarus By Matisse
(Inspired by the painting)

Flying past the stars he goes
Falling through the air he soars
His legs floating in the midnight air
His heart pounding like a burst balloon.
The sun blazes in the sky
His eyes are a blur passing by
The black shiny shadow in the distance.
He tumbles down like a heavy rock,
Stars glittering around him in the midnight sky
Everything is silent.

Jessica Price (11)
Nicol Mere Primary School, Wigan

The World

World, world is so wonderful,
World, world is so good.
World, world is so blue,
World, world is so colourful,
World, world, there are so many countries in it too!

Kendell Webb (9)
Our Lady of the Assumption School, Blackpool

The World

The world is great
The world is fine
I wish it could be mine, mine, mine!
France, Italy, Germany and Finland,
But of course my favourite is England!

Charlie Smith (9)
Our Lady of the Assumption School, Blackpool

The World

The world is great
The world is fine
The world is cool
And so am I.

Emily Maguire (8)
Our Lady of the Assumption School, Blackpool

The World

The world is calm
The world is great
The world is something
You can't hate.

Marcus Wall (9)
Our Lady of the Assumption School, Blackpool

Fantastic World

Fantastic world
nothing can replace this fantastic world
the sun is on the left
the sun is on the right
the sun is always shining bright.
The moon is gleaming in the foggy night
the trees sway in the wind.
This is a great, fantastic, beautiful
and colourful world.

Teresa Amatiello (9)
Our Lady of the Assumption School, Blackpool

Love

Love sounds like the beat of a heart
the colour is red as a tart
it tastes like a kiss running in my throat
romance is riding in a boat
love smells like an oak
it feels like wearing my best coat.

Ron Gregory-Clark (7)
Polperro School, Looe

Fun, Love, Anger

Fun feels like smooth silk,
Fun feels like nice warm milk,
Love sounds like the sway of the breeze,
Love sounds like the squirrels in the trees,
Anger reminds me of an angry clone,
Anger reminds me of a dark, cold stone.

Chloe Reeves (8)
Polperro School, Looe

Fun

Fun tastes like spaghetti
Fun smells like chips
Fun reminds me of holidays
Fun is riding a horse.

Lucy Jones (7)
Polperro School, Looe

Sadness

It feels like a person
It smells like air
It tastes like invisibility
It reminds me about care.

Daniel Lee Clowes (7)
Polperro School, Looe

Silence

Silence is like white
Silence is like no one's there
Silence is like a dog dreaming
Silence is like school.

Jack Merriott (7)
Polperro School, Looe

Darkness

Darkness feels like cold wind,
Darkness tastes like spookiness,
Darkness feels like snakes.

Oliver Dobbs (7)
Polperro School, Looe

Anger

Anger reminds me of chillies
It reminds me of fire
It reminds me of burning wood
It reminds me of burning chips
It reminds me of hot waffles.

Patrick Small (7)
Polperro School, Looe

Happiness

Happiness smells like sweets
Happiness reminds me of fairs
Happiness is blue
Happiness sounds like fun.

Rose Pipkin (7)
Polperro School, Looe

Happiness

Makes me feel like air,
It is green like a flower,
It smells like red roses in a field,
It tastes like tomato ketchup.

Alexander Butters (7)
Polperro School, Looe

Happiness

Happiness smells like chocolate,
Happiness tastes like sweets,
Happiness feels like sponge,
Happiness looks like fun.

Tom Humphries (6)
Polperro School, Looe

Darkness

Darkness feels like a hot knife going through me
Darkness smells like a burning fire,
Darkness reminds me of ghosts,
Darkness is black,
Darkness sounds like the wind.

Lauren Fisher (7)
Polperro School, Looe

Hate

Hate smells like a boiling sausage,
Hate tastes like chocolate,
Hate sounds like the rough sea,
Hate is black like a dark, black bedroom.

Jordon Puckey (8)
Polperro School, Looe

Darkness

Darkness sounds like the band, 'The Darkness',
Darkness smells like hot burgers off the barbecue,
Darkness is the colour of gold, like money,
Darkness tastes like smoked beef.

Byron Puckey (8)
Polperro School, Looe

Love

Love sounds like God
Love tastes like apples
Love feels like gold
Love reminds me of my grandad.

Megan Tamblyn (8)
Polperro School, Looe

Anger

Anger reminds me of my stepmum,
Anger smells like smoke racing down my body,
Anger reminds me of chillies burning my tongue,
Anger sounds like a very hot steam train,
Anger reminds me of a hideous monster,
Anger tastes like a squashed banana,
Anger is a very dark black.

Joseph Callum Oxley (7)
Polperro School, Looe

Fun

Fun feels like a bald head,
Fun is as green as grass,
It tastes like a hundred muffins,
It sounds like a stupid poem.

Jonathan Lewis (8)
Polperro School, Looe

Darkness

Darkness smells like fresh mint
Darkness tastes like burnt chips
Darkness feels like a big purple blob.

Hayley Alice Bentley (7)
Polperro School, Looe

Anger

Anger smells like a red-hot onion,
Anger smells like a red-hot chilli,
Anger smells like a bowl of fire.

Dillon Hooker (8)
Polperro School, Looe

Love

Love sounds like a bird tweeting
Love sounds like singing, lovely
Love feels like a tingle inside
Love looks like a beautiful show
Love feels like I need to know.

Chloe Jones (8)
Polperro School, Looe

Hate

Hate is like a round fireball
Hate is the colour of a pale person's skin
Hate reminds me of a fox
Hate is similar to anger.

Cameron Brooks (8)
Polperro School, Looe

Sweets

Oh sweet, oh sweet
You're nice to eat.
Oh sweet, oh sweet
You're so neat.
Oh sweet, oh sweet
You need a seat.
Oh sweet, oh sweet
You've got a nice beat.
Oh sweet, oh sweet
You've got a nice smell
Sometimes you even ring like a bell.
Oh sweet, oh sweet
You're the *best* treat!

Rachel Thompson (7)
Redhill Primary School, Derby

Playing In The Playground

Small children running free without a care in the world.
Kids balancing on the climbing frame trying not to fall off.
Juniors kicking footballs through the air into open windows.
Girls skipping and trying to get the most jumps in a row.
Boys wrestling on the grass attempting to throw other boys
                                             on the ground.
A child doing handstands and every time falling on his head.

Joy when it's the beginning of playtime.
Happiness when you score a goal.
Cheerful when you're playing tag with your friends.
Disappointment as the end bell rings.

The cry of an infant as he falls over.
Laughter of juniors when one of them tells a joke.
Teachers shouting at a boy who pushed someone over.
The words, 'Ready or not, here I come.'
Children shouting when they see a fighter plane going past.
Cheers when it's the end of school and it's a weekend.

David Oliver (10)
Red Rose Primary School, Chester-Le-Street

I Want To Paint . . .

I want to paint the summer's day.
I want to paint England winning a football match.
I want to paint me going to a really hot country.
I want to paint me eating chocolate sundae.
I want to paint people diving into hot chocolate.
I want to paint a forest.
I want to paint a baby duckling.
I want to paint fantastic people dancing
I want to paint a pop star.
I want to paint an incredible footballer.

Jennifer Walls (10)
Red Rose Primary School, Chester-Le-Street

Birthday

My uncle called
In the middle of the night
'It's time,' he said, almost crying
My gran woke me up
'It's time,' she whispered excitedly
'Time for what?' I asked sleepily
'You're going to be a big cousin'
That was the best feeling in my whole life
I wept (with happiness of course)
All the family came round
We all sat in the front room
Impatiently.
'It's been a long nine months,' I said
To break the silence
'I agree,' my father answered
The phone rang again
I answered
'She's born and beautiful,'
My uncle cried
By this point
I was dancing around the house shouting

'She's here, she's here!'

Holly Neave (10)
Red Rose Primary School, Chester-Le-Street

I Want To Paint . . .

I want to paint me playing for Newcastle and scoring lots of goals
I want to paint me playing with Alan Shearer and being the
best captain
I want to paint me and the best food in the world and eat it up
I want to paint a big boy and play cool games with him
I want to paint like an artist
I want to paint me with 100,000 shining diamonds.

Robbie Hall (9)
Red Rose Primary School, Chester-Le-Street

Templeton In The Barn

(Inspired by 'Charlotte's Web' by E B White)

A swallow swerving past the window
The goose and goslings waddling by
Mr Zuckerman and Lurvey admiring Wilbur
Fern sitting on a milking stool in the sheep fold
Rain trickling down off the roof after last night's storm
Wilbur showing off to admirers
Avery on the swing rope
Mrs Zuckerman in the kitchen chopping carrots
The spiderlings weaving a web
Mr and Mrs Arable driving up the road
The goose and goslings honking away
Mr Zuckerman and Lurvey doing business
Birds singing sweet songs
Children playing on the grass
The barn door creaking
My tummy rumbling
Wilbur eating, acting famished
Angry when I am disturbed
Happy in my own way.

Ryan Jefferson (10)
Red Rose Primary School, Chester-Le-Street

I Want To Paint . . .

I want to paint a baby's first word.
I want to paint my sharing love.
I want to paint a tired, loving, caring doctor.
I want to paint my dad signing his crazy contract.
I want to paint a human's inside.
I want to paint a perfectly accurate man or woman.
I want to paint the smell of melted chocolate, hot, sticky.
I want to paint the last thing in a person's life you know very well.
I want to paint a wonderland that gets on so well.
I want to paint the spiciest curry in the world . . .
And try some.

Lisa Ryan (10)
Red Rose Primary School, Chester-Le-Street

My New Scary School

In July 2000 my mum said,
'You are going to start
Red Rose Primary School.'
I was so scared.
She said to me,
'I know you miss your old school
but it is a new chance to make
new friends.'

There was no time to say
No!
So we set off in the car.
I was nearly sick.
I thought to myself, *what if*
everybody is older than me?
Or . . .
Then my mum said,
'Stop worrying.'

We are here now,
Oh no!

Then a girl called Sarah
came to meet me.
I thought to myself, *this girl is nice.*
I wonder if everybody is as nice
as Sarah is.
I walked to the classroom.

In July 2000 my mum said,
'You are going to start
Red Rose Primary School.'
I was so scared.

Victoria Towler (10)
Red Rose Primary School, Chester-Le-Street

The Joust

I looked at the motley crowd which was punching the air above them.
My lance quivered as I saw my nasty-looking jousting opponent.
He had cruel slits for eyes.
There was no doubt he could scare the toughest person in the world
(Which was probably him).
I felt beads of sticky sweat trickling from my forehead to my breastplate
Down to my toes.
I placed my heavy helmet onto my head.
It was hard to see through my visor so I lifted it up.
I suddenly felt courageous, mighty and strong,
But with another look at my opponent, I was scared.
I could hear the vicious roars of the ogre-like audience
Who wanted a fight
And blood.

Jake Danby (10)
Red Rose Primary School, Chester-Le-Street

My Cousin Maddy

One day while I was at my grandma's house
the doorbell rang, I got excited

I answered the door and in walked my auntie
and my uncle, I got excited.

Me, my mum and my little sister all sat round the kitchen table,
my auntie Sam took a large brown envelope out of her bag.
She gave it to me, I got excited.

I opened it slowly, my eyes were glued to the envelope,
I took out a scan, it was black and white, I got excited.

My auntie Sam said, 'I'm going to have a baby girl,
I think I'll call her Maddy . . .
I got very excited.

Sophie Hodgson (10)
Red Rose Primary School, Chester-Le-Street

Why?

One Saturday morning I went to Tesco with my mum,
when we were coming up the bank
I said,
'I am glad Grandad has not
died yet because I
would like to say
bye to him.'

My mum looked at me in a funny way, I was
scared at that point. I asked my mum,
'Why did you look at me
like that?'
She did not answer me.

I went into the house, my dad and mum told me
and my sister Alison to go into the
living room and made us sit down.

Dad said,
'You know how Grandad is poorly, well
he died last night, he was in a
painful way, he was really
really ill. We will go
to Granny's and go
to the funeral, OK?'

I didn't cry but I had a tear in my eye and
Dad did too. It was Dad's dad.

I was really sad because my cousin had just died as well,
I cried then I thought my mum and
dad were lying but I knew when I
went to my cousin's funeral.

Why did he have to die?
Why?

Jayne Beveridge (9)
Red Rose Primary School, Chester-Le-Street

Time For The Cruise

Every day, counting the days 'til the day of the cruise.
I kept saying to my mam, '136 days . . . 135 days . . .'
How long did it take?
It seemed like years!
Longing for it to come.
I kept wondering what it would be like,
Kept looking in the brochure.
I didn't know what it would be like 'til the day came.
It's come,
It's come.
The cruise ship was massive
With lots of bars and restaurants.
First we went to the bar
Had a *lovely* glass of fruit punch.
We went to the theatre
Every night
And the kids' club
Every day.
I kept saying to my mam,
'It's come,
It's come.'
And
Every day, counting the days, 'til the day of the cruise.
It's come,
It's come,
It's come,
It's come.

Anna Burn (9)
Red Rose Primary School, Chester-Le-Street

The Romans

I can see a mighty Roman army marching to the castle
Archers gripping their bows like madmen
My men running to the gate but burning oil is poured on them.

I feel terrified looking at the sharp point on all the men's swords
Because one of them will put me to my death.

I can hear the roar of the Romans
And the snorting of the horses
The screaming
The screaming
Of my men
Defeat is certain.

Zak Dunster (10)
Red Rose Primary School, Chester-Le-Street

I Want To Paint . . .

I want to paint a roaring motorbike.
I want to paint the future.
I want to paint shining gold coins.
I want to paint the intergalactic space.
I want to paint a time machine.
I want to paint loads of mint games.
I want to paint the past.
I want to paint lots of Warhammer.
I want to paint fireworks exploding.
I want to paint Christmas presents under the tree.

Alastair Usher (10)
Red Rose Primary School, Chester-Le-Street

I Want To Paint . . .

I want to paint the feeling of cool ice cream trickling through my body.
I want to paint the smell of a chocolate-scented rose.
I want to paint the smell of a scorching sun shining over
                                    the Sahara Desert.
I want to paint the feeling of happiness.
I want to paint the feeling of a bird flying for the first time.
I want to paint a baby's first thought.
I want to paint the smell of winning.
I want to paint the smell of snowflakes falling.
I want to paint the smell of a rainbow.
I want to paint the feeling of eating a sticky strawberry marshmallow.

Sarah Donkin (10)
Red Rose Primary School, Chester-Le-Street

I Want To Paint A Poem

I want to paint myself leading out England and Liverpool
football clubs.
I want to paint a leaping leopard running across the dry,
deserted desert.
I want to paint me ruling a country as king.
I want to paint me and my family having the time of our lives in a
Caribbean country.
I want to paint a baby's first word.
I want to paint a panther puffing and panting.
I want to paint a bird's first thought when just coming out of its egg,
looking out to the world.

Steven Jamfrey (10)
Red Rose Primary School, Chester-Le-Street

My Baby Cousin

In January my aunty gave birth to my cousin called Harriet.
Harriet is funny.
She gurgles and blows big bubbles
like all babies do.
She is a cute baby, she weighs a ton
like all babies do.
My uncle, he puts her on the sofa
while he is hoovering.
She has smelly nappies,
like all babies do.
She burps, she cries, she sleeps a lot,
like all babies do.

Connor Bell (10)
Red Rose Primary School, Chester-Le-Street

I Want To Paint A Poem

I want to paint me playing for Sunderland and England.
I want to paint a nice lovely day watching Juventus play Inter Milan.
I want to paint the smell of a lion's breath.
I want to paint the taste of nice Yorkshire puddings.
I want to paint a nice and hot day at the beach.
I want to paint me going to see a Formula One race.
I want to paint me holding the World Cup.
I want to paint me seeing Saturn's gold rings.
I want to paint my dream dinner.
I want to paint me seeing a cheetah.

Alex Miller (10)
Red Rose Primary School, Chester-Le-Street

Tree In The Rainforest

What can you see?
Two jaguar cubs playing fighting
An arrow tree-frog eating flies
Yanomami man climbing a tall tree to get some honey from a beehive
A spider monkey swinging from tree to tree stopping every so often
to eat some fruit
A snake slithering slyly across stones
Bits of fruit that the monkeys have dropped
A monkey-eating eagle chasing an orang-utan dodging all the trees
in its way
A whole family of leaf-cutter ants scuttling backwards and forwards
with bits of leaf
A Yanomami boy picking cherries to paint himself with
An anteater searching for ants on the forest floor.

What can you feel?
The breeze blowing softly at me
A monkey sitting on one of my branches
A lizard climbing up the front of my tree trunk
A bird-eating spider crawling around over my roots
Little ants scuttling around on my branches
Pain as an arrow hits my tree trunk.

What can you hear?
The shouting of triumph from the Yanomami people because
they've just caught a crocodile
The howling of the howler monkey
The beating of a hummingbird's wings
The hissing of a cobra
The screeching sound coming from the monkey-eating eagle
soaring smoothly through the sky
The sound of a jaguar rustling through the leaves
A colourful bird singing softly on the tree.

Zak Cordell (10)
Red Rose Primary School, Chester-Le-Street

Time To Get Acting

Today's the day, the day I'm going to the Gala Theatre,
To perform on stage.
I'm ready with my costumes,
I'm ready for my room number to be called out.
I'm ready.
I'm ready.
I've got inside now, face to face with my room,
Now I'm standing on the carpet to find my place.
I'm ready to perform,
I'm ready for my first costume.
I'm ready.
I'm ready.
I'm in the wings now,
Heading for the stage
I'm ready to dance,
I'm ready.
I'm ready.
I've finished now, getting my things together.
I'm ready to go home,
I'm ready to leave the Gala Theatre.
I'm ready.
I'm . . . ready.

Rebecca Clarke (9)
Red Rose Primary School, Chester-Le-Street

I Want To Paint . . .

I want to paint a drag car racing at speed.
I want to paint a KX motorbike jumping logs.
I want to paint a gangster with his gun.
I want to paint a dog with teeth like razors.
I want to paint a rapper like Tupac Shakur.
I want to paint a guitar called a Gibson.

Jake Henaghan (9)
Red Rose Primary School, Chester-Le-Street

Child In The Playground

As I stand in the playground
I see a little boy on a bench reading a book,
Children are playing football on the concrete.
Girls and boys are making their way round the climbing frame,
Some boys are hanging around with each other.
I feel a ball knocking past my legs.
I am wanting to join the boy reading the book.
I hear children calling from one to another.
Chains are rattling as they are shaken on the climbing frame.

Anthony Beach (9)
Red Rose Primary School, Chester-Le-Street

This Little Horse

This little horse went to Oliver's house
This little horse stayed home
This little horse ate green grass
And this little horse answered the phone
And this little horse goes
Neigh, neigh, neigh
All the way home.

Mansoor Ahmed (9)
Richmond Hill School, Luton

This Little Rabbit

This little rabbit went to Woolworths
This little rabbit went to church
This little rabbit ate a sandwich
And this little rabbit went cluck
And this little rabbit went
Tut, tut, tut
All the way home.

Maddy Ellems (9)
Richmond Hill School, Luton

This Little Cat

This little cat watched DVDs
This little cat climbed a tree
This little cat ate jelly
And this little cat had a baby
And this little cat went
Miaow, miaow, miaow
All the way home.

Karl Fludgate (9)
Richmond Hill School, Luton

This Little Tiger

This little tiger went to Asda
This little tiger stayed at home
This little tiger ate some children
And this little tiger bought a gnome
And this little tiger goes
Roar, roar, roar
All the way home.

Lucy Gates (8)
Richmond Hill School, Luton

This Little Duck

This little duck went swimming
This little duck stayed at home
This little duck went skiing
And this little duck went to Rome
And this little duck went
Quack, quack, quack
All the way home.

Oliver Mills (8)
Richmond Hill School, Luton

This Little Dog

This little dog went to Toys R Us
This little dog stayed at home
This little dog ate chocolate
And this little dog chewed a bone
And this little dog went
Woof, woof, woof
All the way home.

Philip Dines (9)
Richmond Hill School, Luton

This Little Bird

This little bird went to her aunty's house
This little bird went for a walk
This little bird went to the movies
And this little bird bought some chalk
And this little bird went
Tweet, tweet, tweet
All the way home.

Charlotte Simmonds (9)
Richmond Hill School, Luton

This Little Monkey

This little monkey played football
This little monkey scored a goal
This little monkey wanted his mum
And this little monkey went
Ooh, ooh, ooh
All the way home.

Redwan Shafi (8)
Richmond Hill School, Luton

What Am I?

My outside is . . .
like a mowed lawn
as hard as a log
green as grass
tender like a rose
looks like frogs' skin
sticky as glue
ploughed like a field.

My inside is . . .
soft as a sponge
juicy as a pear
squishy as gunge
red as rose
sweet as sugar
squishy as a tomato
red as raw.

I am a watermelon.

Zack Wells (10)
St Bridget's Catholic Primary School, Warrington

What Am I . . . ?

My outside is . . .
hard as a rock
green as an apple
as stripy as a freshly mowed lawn
and as smooth as ice.

My inside is . . .
sticky as glue
and as red as blood
as soft as a big freshly aired pillow.

What am I?
A watermelon.

Samuel Mulholland (10)
St Bridget's Catholic Primary School, Warrington

What Am I?

My outside looks like:
a green moon,
it's a meany greeny,
looks like a frog's skin,
as green as grass,
as hard as rock,
as round as a football,
ploughed like a field,
it's stripy green.

My inside looks like:
it looks like blood red,
when cut up it looks like a mouth,
red as blood,
red as raw,
red as a sunset.
It looks like a cave inside,
juicy as an apple,
seeds as black as a bee's stripes,
it's as sweet as sugar,
tasty as a yummy green,
I am a watermelon.

Louise Mannion (11)
St Bridget's Catholic Primary School, Warrington

What Am I?

My outside is as green as a tortoise shell.
My inside is as red as a strawberry.

The watermelon looks like our school uniform,
The ties and our jumpers are the same as the watermelon.

It is as red as a rose and as sweet as sugar,
Red as blood and delicious as a strawberry and raspberry.

The seeds are spotty like a ladybird.

Kathleen Chua (10)
St Bridget's Catholic Primary School, Warrington

Animal Alphabet

A is for antelope that runs through the field
B is for bear that wears a big shield
C is for cat that wears a big coat
D is for dogs that sail in boats
E is for elephants that get ready for lunch
F is for fish that get ready to punch
G is for gorillas that bang on their chests
H is for hyenas that are little pests
I is for insects that like to crawl
J is for jellyfish that are very small
K is for kangaroo that gets ready for dinner
L is for leeches that make you thinner
M is for mice that like to climb
N is for newt that swims all the time
O is for owls that like to fly
P is for pigs that live in pigsties
Q is for quails that have lovely wings
R is for rhinos that do silly things
S is for snakes that like to bake cakes
T is for turtles that garden with rakes
U is for unicorns that gallop everywhere
W is for worms that like to dare
XYZ are too rare!

Louise Penlington (7)
St Edward's Catholic Primary School, Halton

The Moon

The moon goes cold when the sun goes down.
The sun goes hot when the moon goes down.
The stars go bright when the sun goes down.
The sky goes blue when the stars go down.
The clouds go white when the stars go down.
The birds sing when the sun pops up.
The chickens say cock-a-doodle when the sun pops up.
The spaceship stops time still when the sun pops up.

Craig Ashley (8)
St Edward's Catholic Primary School, Halton

A Fly In The Classroom

Bluebottle, bluebottle
Come flying down

Bluebottle, bluebottle
Turn around

Bluebottle, bluebottle
Land on the ground

Bluebottle, bluebottle
Jump up and down

Bluebottle, bluebottle
What shall we do?

Bluebottle, bluebottle
Play again

Bluebottle, bluebottle
Fly in the sky

Bluebottle, bluebottle
Sting me again

Bluebottle, bluebottle
It doesn't hurt

Bluebottle, bluebottle
Try it again.

Joshua Peck (8)
St Edward's Catholic Primary School, Halton

Skipping Club

Skipping high, skipping low
With Rhiannon and Katherine
So, so, so if I were you
I'd come to my skipping club
Where you can skip all day long
Skipping everywhere through the court
And all you can hear are our shoes tapping, tip and tap
Tip tap, tip tap, tip tap.

Paige Barker (8)
St Edward's Catholic Primary School, Halton

The Funny Alphabet

A is for animals that all go crazy
B is for bananas that peel in half
C is for cats that purr all the time
D is for dogs that bark all day
E is for elephants that get ready for brunch
F is for fish that make fish lunch
G is for guns that go *bang, bang, bang*
H is for hippo that are big and round
I is for insects that sometimes bite
J is for jelly that wobbles in your tum
K is for kittens that like to jump
L is for lions that make loud roars
M is for mice that squeak around the house
N is for newts that swim in the pond
O is for owls that hoot all night
P is for porcupines that spike you
Q is for a queen that sits on the throne
R is for rain that gets you wet
S is for stones that are smooth and round
T is for trumpets that are big and loud
U is for umbrella that keeps you dry
V is for vase that holds beautiful flowers
W is for wind that blows over trees
X is for x-ray that makes a sound
Y is for yacht that is a boat
Z is for zebra that lives in a zoo.

Amy Poole (8)
St Edward's Catholic Primary School, Halton

Flying Teacher

Something happened yesterday
Our class teacher blew away
She was standing by her chair
Then suddenly she wasn't there.

She floated by the class window
Every child pulled her down
They were shouting, 'Yippee
Yippee, yippee.'

Aaron Kirkman (9)
St Edward's Catholic Primary School, Halton

Animals Conga

A is for antelope running through grass
N is for newt swimming in a pond
I is for insects playing in the mud
M is for mouse crawling in the kitchen
A is for ant carrying eggs
L is for leopard bounding through the forest
S is for snake slithering slowly in the sun.

Kadie Brown (8)
St Edward's Catholic Primary School, Halton

Books - Haiku

Delight of reading
Passes every day by me
Great temptation found.

Daniel Curtis (8)
St Joseph's RC Primary School, Matlock

Monsters - Haiku

What's under the bed?
Big, scary monsters creeping
It is almost dawn.

Theresa Hannan (9)
St Joseph's RC Primary School, Matlock

Harry Potter - Haiku

Harry Potter's great
at playing Quidditch matches
and cool wizard games.

Matthew Pilgrim (9)
St Joseph's RC Primary School, Matlock

Football - Haiku

The ground is waiting
waiting for the teams to come
they are nearly here.

Stephen Quinn (9)
St Joseph's RC Primary School, Matlock

Ghosts - Haiku

Ghosts, ghouls all whining
Shocking people from their beds
I am terrified.

Adam O'Shea (8)
St Joseph's RC Primary School, Matlock

Fear - Haiku

Tremble down the spine,
Butterflies in the stomach
Chill sweat on the brow.

Ella Humpston (9)
St Joseph's RC Primary School, Matlock

Fire Flames - Haiku

Fire flames all around
Fire burning paths with fire flames
Guides us through the night.

Matthew Brunt (9)
St Joseph's RC Primary School, Matlock

Flowers - Haiku

Flowers popping up
To see the sun rising up
Snowdrops open up.

Marisa Hepburn (9)
St Joseph's RC Primary School, Matlock

Eagle - Haiku

Swooping low at night,
The eagle comes from the cliff,
Embarking for prey.

Catherine Haworth (9)
St Joseph's RC Primary School, Matlock

Rugby - Haiku

Rugby is the best.
The crowd roar for the great teams.
Rugby rocks the world.

Curtis Bolam & Drew Mullaney (9)
St Joseph's RC Primary School, Matlock

Friends - Haiku

Lots of friends have I.
Big and small and thin and fat.
I'm very lucky.

Natasha Kidd (8)
St Joseph's RC Primary School, Matlock

Swimmers - Haiku

Swimmers swimming now.
It is great and brilliant.
Go swimming today.

Philip Eastwood (9)
St Joseph's RC Primary School, Matlock

Sea - Haiku

Salty waves are blue
Blue sailing boats are drifting
Kids playing beach ball.

Kitty Kenyon (9)
St Joseph's RC Primary School, Matlock

Blue Tit - Haiku

As the sun rises
He sings and chirps all day long
Until the night strikes.

Edward Longville (8)
St Joseph's RC Primary School, Matlock

Anger

Anger looks like red roasting, boiling lava.
Anger sounds like a growling dog.
Anger tastes like a rotting skull.
Anger smells like dead, smelly, minging people.
Anger reminds me of deadly pain.

John Christie (11)
St Margaret's Primary School, Loanhead

Hunger

Hunger feels like a sharp knife slit into your stomach,
Hunger looks like the illusion of food lying before you,
Hunger reminds me of the lovely taste of hot food,
Hunger smells like a distant swoop of air running past your nose,
Hunger tastes like bitter sand when you could eat anything.

Aaron Stenhouse (11)
St Margaret's Primary School, Loanhead

Anger

Anger looks like the blazing red fire from a dragon's mouth
Anger sounds like the rumbling of thunder
Anger tastes like extremely bitter lemons
Anger smells like the smoke from a steam engine
Anger feels like an exploding building.

Connor McLurg (11)
St Margaret's Primary School, Loanhead

Cona And Norma

C overed with a pure white coat,
O ver a pretty face lies huge ears,
N ashing around having fun,
A vote for a funniest dog on earth.

&

N ever wanting to be left alone,
O ver the moon when she sees her master,
R unning about having fun,
M ountains of love inside,
A vote for the cutest dog on earth.

Cameron Ramsay (11)
St Margaret's Primary School, Loanhead

Fun

Fun looks like a happy, cheerful yellowy colour.
Fun smells like lovely, fresh spring air.
Fun tastes like fresh baked cake.
Fun sounds like laughter.
Fun makes you feel happy and excited.
Fun reminds me of people being happy and cheerful.

Reice MacKale (10)
St Margaret's Primary School, Loanhead

Spring

Looks like lambs jumping about in the meadow.
Spring tastes like the crunch of a juicy apple.
Spring smells like cow manure.
Spring sounds like birds singing.
Spring feels like the soft grass in the meadow.
Spring reminds me of sunny weather.

Callum Scott (11)
St Margaret's Primary School, Loanhead

Anger

Anger looks like hot boiling blood of a dragon's skin.
Anger sounds like a lion hunting its prey.
Anger tastes like the bitterness of chemical gas.
Anger smells like garlic spilling out over the world.
Anger feels like a crown of thorns on your head.
Anger reminds me of the blood boiling temperature rumbling
                                                    in my body.
Anger speaks as though the world cannot talk again.
Anger is as evil as Satan himself.
Anger is a mind-bubbling thing.
Anger moves like a racehorse around in your head.

Christopher Black (11)
St Margaret's Primary School, Loanhead

Silence!

Silence looks like a feather falling from a bird in flight.
Silence sounds like a distant whisper coming from over the horizon.
Silence tastes like a fresh stick of fluffy white candyfloss.
Silence smells like a new bottle of perfume from a shop.
Silence feels like baby rabbits' fur.
Silence reminds me of cotton wool wrapped tightly around
                                            an antique vase.

Lisa White (12)
St Margaret's Primary School, Loanhead

Fear

Fear feels like a following shadow creeping up behind you.
Fear smells like an open fire crackling in the wind,.
Fear tastes like sour milk in your breakfast cereal.
Fear looks like a razor-sharp blade cutting on your cheeks.
Fear sounds like the aching pain of cramp in your legs.
Fear reminds me of dark alley way in the coldness of the night.

Nicole Steadwood (11)
St Margaret's Primary School, Loanhead

Fear

Fear sounds like a freaky, frightful ghost whispering through your ear.
Fear tastes like coffee, as cold as ice.
Fear feels like hovering through a graveyard where wind shouts at you,
'Go away.'
Fear looks like a venomous viper looking you in the face.
Fear smells like an exploding toxic volcano as hot as the sun
on your nose.
Fear reminds me of my bad dreams coming alive.

Iain Ramsay (12)
St Margaret's Primary School, Loanhead

Love

Love smells like the sweet smell of a red rose.
Love feels like a super soft kiss on the nose.
Love reminds me of the wonderful warm feeling you get inside
When you sit and watch the tide.
Love tastes like a sweet strawberry.
Love is the sound of a romantic ferry.

Rachael Dalgetty (11)
St Margaret's Primary School, Loanhead

Love

Love is like pink champagne,
Love is the soft sound of kisses over and over again,
Love tastes like green grapes that have just been picked
And the sweet smell of vanilla ice cream that hasn't been licked,
Love feels like the warm sun in the sky,
And reminds me of my beautiful beloved baby cousin Tom.

Lucy Denholm (12)
St Margaret's Primary School, Loanhead

Darkness

Darkness you see more and more of,
Darkness is a trap you know of,
Darkness covers up half the world,
And it makes hedgehogs get more curled and curled.

Darkness can be starlight,
Darkness can be moonlight,
But nothing can change
That darkness will always be darkness.

Darkness falls at every night,
And then the sun goes out of sight,
After midnight in comes a little light,
And then when morning comes
Off goes the darkness until tonight.

Bonamy Tetteh-Lartey (10)
St Margaret's Primary School, Loanhead

Fear!

Fear is like a room full of fierce Rottweilers waiting to sink
the sharpness of their teeth into you, like a mysterious shark
that hunts beneath the waves.
Fear looks like darkness of a lonely alleyway which doesn't like visitors.
Fear tastes like the bitterness of flowing blood spitting
out of your stomach when you have just been brutally attacked.
Fear smells like the cold and damp walls of an abandoned tunnel.
Fear feels like the vicious spike of sharp barbed wire.
Fear reminds me of looking down the barrel of a gun
waiting for the trigger to be pulled.
The only thing to fear is fear *itself!*

Samantha Rush (11)
St Margaret's Primary School, Loanhead

The Beast Called Anger

Anger is like a beast unleashing inside you,
Anger feels like a fiery hot demon poking you in the back with a stick,
Anger sounds like the screaming of someone getting murdered,
Anger looks like an angry bulldog protecting its territory
when you look into its eyes,
Anger smells like the steam from a bull's nose
before it's about to charge,
Anger tastes like the bitterness of Hell.

Marcos Koulis (11)
St Margaret's Primary School, Loanhead

Darkness

Darkness is black and it smells like a mouse
And there is nothing to hear
Reeking damp smell is what it smells like
Darkness tastes like toxic waste
It feels like you are in a stone cold bath with snakes in it
Darkness reminds me of the way I was relaxing in a jacuzzi
And all the other relaxing things I have done in my life
Darkness is fun to play hide-and-seek in.

John Bain (10)
St Margaret's Primary School, Loanhead

Fear

Fear looks black like a gun waiting to shoot
Fear sounds like a flying bullet going past your head
Fear tastes like blood going down your throat
Fear smells like cold sweat
Fear feels like being dragged down a hall
Fear reminds me of living on the streets.

Sean Anderson (11)
St Margaret's Primary School, Loanhead

At War

What I can see . . .
I can see the flying of the cannons,
The bullets flying all around,
Army tanks rolling from side to side,
The big army bombs above us.

What I feel . . .
Sad about missing my family,
Weary because I'm tired,
Friendless because I don't know anyone,
Lonely because everyone has died.

What I can hear . . .
I can hear the crashing of the bombs,
Shooting like a machine with a lot of noise,
The rumble of planes above us,
The sound of exploding tanks.

Ryan Robinson (10)
St Teresa's Catholic Primary School, St Helens

War

Bombs blasting overhead
One hit and I'll be dead
Leaping flames and fire flashes
Consume the plane which dives and crashes.

Night falls, bullets fly high
Over the hills and under the sky
Then come back down again
Off to kill so many men.

The bullet shot once flew
The bullet shot waits for you
The war is finished
I'm alive
The war is finished
But some didn't survive . . .

Michael Atherton (11)
St Teresa's Catholic Primary School, St Helens

At War

All silence in the town
Only the howling of a dog
The soldiers wait and wait long.

Until someone does a slight cough
Bombs go off
And make raging booms.

Guns bring a pain to your ear
While everyone waits in fear
Soldiers scream as they get hit

Sometimes they go into fits
Planes whiz as they drop bombs overhead
'We're going to die,' that's what they all said.

Screeching of the truck's tyres
Stopping in front of fires
And all these brave men fighting at the front line
They're fighting not wasting any precious time.

Luke James (11)
St Teresa's Catholic Primary School, St Helens

Environment

What can you see?
I see a big, fat, squawking bird looking at me.
What else can you see?
Well, I see a lot fish in the sea.
What do you hear?
I hear people crushing cans.
What do you hear?
I hear people shouting, *'Cancer bands!'*
What else do you hear?
I hear someone smashing a window.
What do you feel?
I feel warm, snuggled and fantastic.

Kayleigh Leyden (11)
St Teresa's Catholic Primary School, St Helens

Transport

I can see
Zooming cars and aeroplanes
Buses and boats
Are all the same
I can see helicopters
Coaches and speed boats
All speeding around me
I can see
Trams, submarines
And trains all around
I feel happy
Sad, sick and tired.
I hear the rumble of
The plane's engines
The speed boats
Swishing on the water
The splash
When the submarine
Goes down.

Emily Hughes (11)
St Teresa's Catholic Primary School, St Helens

Transport

I can see cars stopping and going
And aeroplanes flying over my head
And coaches on the road instead
The buses taking people somewhere
Up in town and to the fair

I feel sick on the aeroplane
And happy when I'm going to a place I like
And I'm annoyed when I go to a place I hate

I can hear the screeching of brakes
Brum of engines
Tick of indicators
And a beep of a horn.

Martin Howard (11)
St Teresa's Catholic Primary School, St Helens

Young Writers - Playground Poets Poems From The UK

The Environment

What do you hear?
The crash of cans.
The flicker of lights,
The bang of doors,
The tear of paper.

What do you see?
I see people recycling.
I can see the pretty flowers
And the nature.
I can see litter on the floor.
I can see a dead animal.

What do you feel like?
I feel happy with nature.
I feel good when we save energy.
I feel excellent when the plants grow.
I feel angry when plants get trodden on.

Joanna Bebbington (11)
St Teresa's Catholic Primary School, St Helens

War

I can see people diving for the floor
The blood on an old man's shorts
People dead on the floor
People running through the door . . .

I can hear people screaming
Men yelling
The men's guns banging
Tanks moving in the trees,
Waiting to explode someone.

I feel like everyone is counting on me
I feel like I am a hero
Because I have saved lots of people
But I am scared of being shot!

Liam Oakshott (11)
St Teresa's Catholic Primary School, St Helens

Soldiers At War

What can they see?
Soldiers can see things in the air,
Blood and dead people and people dying,
Guns and heavy machinery,
Soldiers flying and crying,
Violence around them with no peace.
What can they hear?
Bombs and blasts, cries of pain and flying planes,
Bullets and bits of metal falling off the machines,
The clatter of guns reloading,
Soldiers screaming.
What are they feeling?
Soldiers everywhere feeling quite terrified,
Worried, sick with fear, sad and miserable,
About to die with a shot in the heart.
What can they smell?
Soldiers all smell blood and guts,
Body bits that are rotting,
Burnt metal, smoke and deadly gas.
How do they get around?
Soldiers in bases in crashed planes,
Ships and in tanks and in ditches,
But most on foot.
What are they wearing?
Soldiers and colonels all wearing green,
To camouflage them so they can't be seen.

Emily Talau (11)
St Teresa's Catholic Primary School, St Helens

Transport

What can I see?
Zooming cars and jet planes,
Bashing into cranes,
Lorries trudging along,
That are very, very long.

What can I smell?
The sweet lemony air freshener,
Leaving the aroma in my hair,
Ghastly exhaust fumes,
Polluting a pontoon.

What can I hear?
Lorries' horns going
Beep,
Cars going past
Yelling sheep.
The vroom of a plane passing by,
The chopping of a helicopter fly, fly, fly!

What can I touch?
The smooth sensation of the side of the car,
The sharp edge of the propellers on the helicopter,
A rough tyre on a lorry,
The comfy back seat, sleep now,
Sorry.

Jessica Leather (11)
St Teresa's Catholic Primary School, St Helens

War

What can I see?
Explosions of bombs
Up above
Planes swoop down
Like a graceful dove
Men at war
Fighting for their lives
Children in the shelter
With the wives.
What do I feel?
Upset that my dad has gone
And won't be back
For long
Mad with people
Telling a lie
Afraid that my family
Might die.

Joe Snee (10)
St Teresa's Catholic Primary School, St Helens

The Environment

Children running round and round
Kids crying on the ground
You've had a fight with your best friend
Nowhere to play.

I can hear . . .
The laughter of children
The screaming of the kids
The clatter of the feet
The whistle blowing telling you to get in.

You feel sad and lonely
You've got no friends
Got no place to go
Nowhere else to go
And play.

Patrick Tobin (11)
St Teresa's Catholic Primary School, St Helens

Erica's Story

I do not know my birth name
I do not know my birth date
What I do know is, when I was just a few months old,
My mother threw me to life.
God said that my people would be as many as
The stars in the heavens
Six million of my people
Were gassed, burned and tortured.
Many died of starvation.
Starved of food, water, sleep,
Belongings, families, homes
And freedom.
They were robbed of everything
They were robbed of life itself,
But not me.
My star still shines.

Elizabeth McCrory (9)
Sacred Heart RC Primary School, Leigh

A Mother's Love

Would a mother
Care for you so much
She could lose you
On her way to death?
Mine did.

Should a mother
Be forced onto a train,
Horrified and in tears,
Hearing the door barred shut?
Mine was.

Could a mother
Be split up from her family,
Knowing that she was going to die,
Travel in agony?
Yes.

Dylan Alexander (9)
Sacred Heart RC Primary School, Leigh

In The Picture

Would a mother flood her baby with tears,
Spread our barbed wire barriers,
Throw her baby to a chance of life?
Mine did.

Would a mother suffer the loss of her baby,
Cover it in kisses
And cry until her death?
Mine did.

Should a mother be relocated to a ghetto,
Left with nothing to feed on
But anguish?
Mine did.

Should a mother
Be taken to a death camp
To be among six million people
Shot, burned, gassed?
If she survived she'd be a walking skeleton.
Mine was.

Liam Stridgeon (9)
Sacred Heart RC Primary School, Leigh

The City Flourishing; Tanabath Festival

(Inspired by the painting 'The City Flourishing; Tanabath Festival' by Ando Hiroshige)

Trees blowing in the wind,
Sand spinning on the ground
Like a little whirlwind.

Feel the wind against your body.
Hear the branches dashing together,
The mountain erupting.

Smell the dust
And the fruit on the trees.
Taste the dust and the fruit.

Matthew Merwin (11)
Sacred Heart RC Primary School, Leigh

Young Writers - Playground Poets Poems From The UK

Would A Mother . . .

Would a mother
Throw you from the window of a train,
Leave you to live your own life?
Mine did.

Should mothers
Have Nazis beat them,
Not know where they are going,
Be separated from their families
And never see them again?

Should people
Be sent to death camps,
Be suffocated in gas chambers,
Have their stars fall from the sky?

Could people
Have been persecuted in the holocaust,
Lived as walking skeletons
With the rest of the world not knowing?
Yes!

Louise Pemberton (9)
Sacred Heart RC Primary School, Leigh

Dynamism Of A Dog On A Leash

(Inspired by the painting 'Dynamism of a Dog on a Leash' by Giacomo Balla)

Tail flapping
Like a flag in the wind.

Leash cracking
Like a whip.

Dog panting
Like a steam train
Puffing smoke.

Stones falling
Behind its paws.

Justin Beacall (11)
Sacred Heart RC Primary School, Leigh

Erika's Story

On her way to death
My mother threw me to life.
I landed on the pale green grass
By me, stood a man with his bike
He picked me up and gave me to a lady near him.
The lady took me from the man
She then looked after me.
She fed me,
Clothed me,
Gave me a birth date,
Took me to school
And gave me a name.
My name is Erika
When I was 21
I found a perfect and beautiful husband
We had 3 children.
They all have children now.
My tree has roots,
My star still shines.

Jemma Morrissey (9)
Sacred Heart RC Primary School, Leigh

Photo Of Penny

A dog in the garden,
Slim and fit.
Little, funny and young.
Liked to play catch,
Loved to walk.
Got lost
And now I only see her
In this picture.
My Penny.
A good dog.
Lost forever.

Molly Marsh (10)
Sacred Heart RC Primary School, Leigh

Would A Mother?

Would a mother
Hug her baby tight,
Then throw her from a train?
Mine did.

Could a mother
Withstand the terrified cries
In the dim light of a cattle car?
Mine did.

Should a mother
Realise her fate
Is to be starved, gassed or shot?
Mine did.

Would a mother
On her way to death,
Throw her baby to life?
Mine did.

Conor McGuinness (9)
Sacred Heart RC Primary School, Leigh

Mary's Story

I'm Jesus' mother,
They call me Mary.
I watched my son
And I sadly, sadly cried.
I was with him for those final minutes,
How long those minutes were.
They brought him to the hilltop
Stripped off all his clothes,
They nailed him to the cross
And he slowly, slowly died.
No one cared for him,
There was nothing I could do
As the sky went black.

Hannah Ridley (10)
Sacred Heart RC Primary School, Leigh

Erika's Story

Would a mother
Wash you in her kisses
Cry her heart out while holding you tight
And throw you off a train?
Mine did.
Would a mother
Say goodbye to her baby,
Never see it again,
So it would survive?
Mine did.
Could you imagine people being
Starved,
Burned,
Gassed?
My people were.
Would people
Go through so much pain and panic
Just because of their religion?
Pushed by Nazis,
Split up from their family and friends,
Forced out of their homes,
Yes!

Shannon Urmston (9)
Sacred Heart RC Primary School, Leigh

In The Picture

Would a mother
Throw you from a train,
Wash you in salty tears,
Save your life?

Mine did.

Would a mother
Starve on a train,
Stand on a train,
Be crushed on a train?

Mine did.

Should a mother
Be stuck in a dim cattle cart,
Be treated badly by German soldiers,
Be forced out of her home?

Mine was.

Should a mother
Be persecuted,
Be tortured because of her religion
Or be killed because someone said so?

Mine was.

Lewis Parr (9)
Sacred Heart RC Primary School, Leigh

Erika's Story

Would a mother
Throw you from a train
Protect you from the stench
Pray that you would live?
Mine did.
Could you imagine
People being crammed into a cattle cart with fear
Legs shaking because of the horror
Broken away from their families?
They were.
Could people
Be sent to horrifying death camps
Because someone said so
Be persecuted, killed for no reason?
They were.
Why did we
Not know what had been going on?
Persecution, torture and death.
Once again my tree has roots
Because of my mother.

Jessica Causby (8)
Sacred Heart RC Primary School, Leigh

This Picture

A soldier in uniform
Wearing his medals.
He's tall,
Brawny-chested.
Fit, young and proud.
That was then.
Now he's sitting in an old people's home
In an armchair
Being treated differently.
An old man.
It's me.

Joe Whittle (10)
Sacred Heart RC Primary School, Leigh

The Stonebreaker

Above the sun is shining
Flowers swaying all around,
Trees are swishing side to side
But his eyes are looking down.
Bang! Bang! Bang!

The boy can see
That his dog wants to play.
'Not yet,' he says,
'Maybe another day.'
Bang! Bang! Bang!

His hand is aching,
His belly is rumbling,
But he must make
The rocks go tumbling.
Bang! Bang! Bang!

He works so hard,
He works all day,
Although he's tired
He's got to stay.
Bang! Bang! Bang!

Sarah France (8)
Sacred Heart RC Primary School, Leigh

A Soldier's Story

I nailed him to the cross.
I sinned against him.
I nailed him to the cross.
I made God angry.
I nailed him to the cross.
I made the sky go black.
I nailed him to the cross.
I wish it was not so.
I nailed him to the cross.
I carry the guilt.

Duncan Boyter (9)
Sacred Heart RC Primary School, Leigh

Swimming In The Ocean

Swimming in the ocean
What did I see?
A big fat turtle
Coming for me.

Swimming in the ocean
What did I see?
A thin spotty eel
Zooming past me.

Swimming in the ocean
What did I see?
A floppy jellyfish
Trying to sting me.

Swimming in the ocean
What did I see?
A small orange starfish
Looking at me.

Swimming in the ocean
What did I see?
A rainbow-coloured parrot fish
Coming to me.

Swimming in the ocean
What did I see?
A black and yellow angelfish
Gliding past me.

Nicola Baczynski (8)
Sacred Heart RC Primary School, Leigh

My Mum

She was
A girl who became
A woman,
A wife,
A mother,
A widow.

She was
The perfect daughter,
Teacher's pet,
Annoying sibling.

She was
Brilliant at painting,
Not too bothered about money,
Only that her paintings sold,
A woman who enjoyed the park.

She was
Delighted when she saw her sisters.
Stuttering sometimes,
Hands trembling
As she thought of her husband.

She was
Always ready to talk
Yet still and cautious.

She was
My mum.

Jennifer Boardman (11)
Sacred Heart RC Primary School, Leigh

Mrs Mounter

(Inspired by the painting 'Mrs Mounter' by Harold Gilman)

A happy girl who became
A scared old woman,
A frightened old lady
Who never went out.

Once a clever schoolgirl,
A talented teenager,
A brilliant writer.
Now,
A frail old woman.

A helpful neighbour,
Someone to rely on.
Friendly,
Always something to say.
Now, who is there to talk to?

A woman who wished
For happiness,
For love,
For more money.
Who wanted her wishes to come true,
But none of them did.
Now she wishes no more.

Victoria Parkinson (11)
Sacred Heart RC Primary School, Leigh

Mrs Mounter

((Inspired by the painting 'Mrs Mounter' by Harold Gilman)

Poor old Mrs Mounter,
All alone,
No family, no friends.
Every day she sits in her chair
Listening to the birds and the wind,
Drinking tea and knitting.

Poor old Mrs Mounter,
You only hear her croaky voice
When she shouts at the children,
'Spoiled kids! Get away from here!
Never had kids, never want 'em.'

Poor old Mrs Mounter,
All alone in her poky flat,
Always a mess, no point in cleaning.
Never goes out,
Phone never rings.

Poor old Mrs Mounter,
Eyes tired and blue,
Cheeks lifeless and colourless
Veins on her hands popping through.

Rachel Heneghan (11)
Sacred Heart RC Primary School, Leigh

Gran

This is really hard for me.
My life has fallen apart,
The greatest gran is dead.

I remember
As a baby she would carry me,
Play with me,
Hold me.
I thought she would always be beside me.

I remember
As a toddler she would shop with me,
Buy things for me,
Do things for me.
I thought she would always be beside me.

I remember
As a child she would go away with me,
Go dancing with me,
Go to school with me.
I thought she would always be beside me.

I remember
As a teen she would kiss me,
Hug me,
Comfort me.
I thought she would always be beside me.

I remember
As an adult she got ill in front of me,
Withered away next to me,
Died before my eyes
And now she is always beside me.

Rebecca Hodkinson (11)
Sacred Heart RC Primary School, Leigh

A Memory

Light grey hair and wrinkled face,
Welcoming sky-blue eyes.
Soft peach skin
Comforting to touch.

I remember
Her long, naturally pink nails
With pearl-white tips.
Her hands as soft as silk.
Always the smell of lemons.
Every day she went shopping
And bought me a chocolate bar from the market.
Lying in her garden every summer,
Reading a good book,
Sipping freshly made lemon juice.

I remember
Going round to her house
Every Saturday with my mum,
Reading her a poem
Or from her favourite, 'Romeo and Juliet'.
I remember, as well,
The day of her funeral.
She looked like she was asleep,
Except I knew
She would never wake up.

Danielle Acton (11)
Sacred Heart RC Primary School, Leigh

From The Old Album

A woman holding a baby girl.
Young.
Smart.
Happy.
Proud but tired.
She loved that baby girl
And enjoyed her work.
She lived in that house
Where my mum grew up.
I loved that house.
I wish I could go back,
But the house was sold.
The woman has died.
The woman was my grandma
Holding my mum.
Now I hold them in my hand.

Jodie Baczynski (10)
Sacred Heart RC Primary School, Leigh

Sun

(Inspired by the 'Weather Series' by David Hockney)

I see the sunlight
Like a thousand light bulbs
Shining with all their might.
I see the flower growing towards the sun.

I feel the heat on the smooth blue cupboard,
The prickly plant
Sharp as the blade from a sharpener.

I hear the birds singing
Like it's their best day of the year.
The cars on the motorway,
The animals running
Their feet sounding like pencils tapping on a table.
Hear the waterfall roar
Like a jet flying past.

Nicholas Ryan (11)
Sacred Heart RC Primary School, Leigh

Judas' Story

I am Judas
I did this,
I gave him the kiss.
Jesus did nothing wrong.

It's not right
That he should suffer.
I did not want this.
Jesus did nothing wrong.

Now I see his pain.
Without him it won't be the same.
I don't know what I've done,
Jesus did nothing wrong.

I look at him and think
It should be me up there.
Why did I give him that kiss?
Jesus did nothing wrong.

Adam Ahmed (10)
Sacred Heart RC Primary School, Leigh

Erika's Poem

Would a mother
Save her daughter's life,
Throw her baby out of a window?
Mine did.

Should a mother suffer
The stench of disease
And watch horrible things done to Jews?
Mine did.

Would a mother say, 'I love you.'
Give you life
And a heart of gold?
Mine did.

Alex Monaghan (9)
Sacred Heart RC Primary School, Leigh

Would A Mother?

Would a mother
Wash you in salted tears,
Throw you from a train
To save your life?
Mine did.

Could you imagine
People being starved,
Catching typhus,
Being crammed into cattle cars
Feeling frightened and shaking,
Hearing whispered rumours of death camps
And the world did not see?

Were people
Tormented and tortured,
Ordered from homes to ghettos
Because of their religion?
Yes!

Could a mother
Save you from this?
Yes!
My star still shines.

Katie Blakeley (9)
Sacred Heart RC Primary School, Leigh

The Two Nuns

(Inspired by the painting 'The Two Nuns' by Noel Coward)

See the people
Bunched up like grapes.
Beach umbrellas like lollipops.

Feel the sand and water
Between your toes.

Hear quiet breezes blowing
Across the sand.
Waves crashing
On the rocks.

Smell the suncream,
Burgers and hot dogs.

Taste the saltwater,
Gritty sand
Blowing in your mouth.

Seaside.

Callum Smith (11)
Sacred Heart RC Primary School, Leigh

Open The Door

(Based on 'The Door' by Miroslav Holub)

Go and open the door
Maybe there is a leech laying on a beach
Maybe there is as squirrel kicking a football
Maybe there is a mole digging up a hole
Maybe there is an astronaut ready for take-off in his rocket.
Maybe . . .

Jack Bushell (8)
Spring Meadow Primary School, Dovercourt

Go And Open The Door

(Based on 'The Door' by Miroslav Holub)

Go and open the door

Maybe there is a witch
playing chase on the football pitch.

Maybe there is a frog
resting on a big fat log.

Maybe there is a nut
falling on my butt.

Maybe there is a boy starting to rumble
I think he needs his apple crumble.

Maybe there is a door
that's very, very poor.

Maybe there is a man
as big as a pan.

Maybe . . .

Justin Cook (8)
Spring Meadow Primary School, Dovercourt

Go And Open The Door

(Based on 'The Door' by Mirolsav Holub)

Go and open the door
Maybe there's a pilot flying a plane
Over a pebbly, wet, sandy beach.
Maybe there's a bunch of children
Playing in a playground.
Maybe there might even be a zoo
With cheeky monkeys in it.
Maybe there might even be a bunch of adults
Chatting away, in the club.
Maybe . . .
You never know.

Molly Ling (8)
Spring Meadow Primary School, Dovercourt

Don't You Dare

'Don't you dare
let the rabbit out of the hutch
while I'm out!' said my mum.

But I did,
as soon as she was out
I opened the latch
and lifted out the rabbit.

She wriggled for a moment,
so I put her on the grass.
She shot off down the garden
I raced after her
but she was too fast for me.
Oh no, I'm in trouble!

Lauren Monger (9)
Spring Meadow Primary School, Dovercourt

Open The Door

(Based on 'The Door' by Miroslav Holub)

Open the door

Maybe there is a white horse standing on my doorstep
waiting to be ridden.

Maybe there is a unicorn
running across the sea.

Maybe there is a ballerina
dancing with a twizzle.

Maybe there is a cat
miaowing for some food.

Maybe . . .

Lauren Mann (9)
Spring Meadow Primary School, Dovercourt

Open The Door

(Based on 'The Door' by Miroslav Holub)

Go and open the door

Maybe there is a toy shop
where there are lots of toys for you.

Maybe there's a mansion with a ghost
who says, 'Boo!'

Maybe there is a palace with the Queen
having tea.

Maybe there is a swimming pool
with a whale having his dinner.

Maybe there is a garden
covered with pink and purple flowers.

Bethany Shears (9)
Spring Meadow Primary School, Dovercourt

Don't You Dare

'Don't you dare
Let the bird out of its cage
While I'm out,' said Mum
But I did
As soon as she'd shut the door
I undid the latch
And the bird flew around the room!
I tried to catch it but it flew higher
And out of the window.
I knew I was in for it!

Steffi Gordon (8)
Spring Meadow Primary School, Dovercourt

Don't You Dare

'Don't you dare
Let that dog out of the pen
When I am out,'
Said my mum

But I did!
As soon as she walked out the door
I let my beautiful dog out of the pen
And played with her
But the kitchen door was open
She ran out of the back door
I raced after her
But she dug a hole
And ran onto the road
I knew I was done for!

Danielle Roberts (9)
Spring Meadow Primary School, Dovercourt

Don't You Dare

'Don't you dare
Let the hamster out of the cage,'
Said Mum
But I did!
As soon as she was out
It was racing across the floor
I went to get the ball
I went chasing, it was too fast
Then the hamster went under the chair
Then I heard my mum
I quickly lifted the chair and got it
I knew I was in for it!

Brandon Button (9)
Spring Meadow Primary School, Dovercourt

Go And Open The Door

(Based on 'The Door' by Miroslav Holub)

Go and open the door
Maybe . . .
There is a snail as big as a whale.
Maybe . . .
There is a hat as big as a cat.
Maybe . . .
There is a cat sitting on a map.
Maybe . . .
There is a snail making a trail.
Maybe . . .
There is a witch playing on a football pitch.

Danielle Pudney (9)
Spring Meadow Primary School, Dovercourt

Don't You Dare

'Don't you dare
Go in my room
While I'm out,' said my mum.

But I did
As soon as she went out
I raced in
I saw lots of presents
I just knew they were for me
I ripped off all the paper
And started playing with my presents
I heard the door go
I just knew I was in trouble.

Alexandra Ramplin (9)
Spring Meadow Primary School, Dovercourt

Open The Door

(Based on 'The Door' by Miroslav Holub)

Open the door
Maybe there is an army of robots taking over the world.
Maybe there are some bombs going to hit a house.
Maybe there is a boat sinking in the rough sea.
Maybe there is a house being built of wood.
Maybe there is a plane in the sky doing stunts.
Maybe . . .

Bengamin Smith (8)
Spring Meadow Primary School, Dovercourt

The Man That Fears Nothing

His hair is pitch-black,
Like the forbidden areas of space.

His bold head is like
The domes of the mosques.

His nose snorts,
Like bulls ready to fight.

His mouth is a locked chamber,
That keeps all secrets in.

His head is a ball,
That bounces when angry.

The white top he wears
Is as white as the stars.

He is a throne,
Unbreakable no matter what.

He is as lazy as a lion,
That sleeps most of the day.

He is a shark,
That fears nothing.

Cagla Bicer (10)
Stamford Hill Primary School, Tottenham

Heaven

The fields are green with petals around them
And geraniums nearby
With children adoring it
For what is life?
Sunflowers are starting to grow.
I walk through the fields
And I feel the cold breeze
Blowing through me
With gentle buzzing towards me
I feel delighted to be here
And have fun with the animals
Because if I was on Earth
It would never be like this
So all I know is
I am in Heaven.

Nicole Davis (11)
Stamford Hill Primary School, Tottenham

A Shadow Sculpture

Life to this beast is not an option
It is a disastrous being
That if released
It would kill him quickly.

His soul is a fiery chamber
Filled with the darkest secrets
That if spilt
Would spread a plague
That would destroy the Earth.

His eyes are a spoilt Earth
That if looked at
Would shatter your brain into a thousand pieces.

David Slater (11)
Stamford Hill Primary School, Tottenham

The King Of Death

His life is the darkest of all,
Filled with grief,
Over killing his own family,
Led by darkness and despair,
His mind burning with flames of Hell,
He is a plague
Sweeping the Earth,
Like icy cold mountain air,
Destroying all that is touched,
Leading all of mankind,
Into flames of darkness,
He carries them,
Through a deadly fire,
But don't be fooled,
For he will surely bring,
Chaos and destruction,
Unless you stop him,
All else is lost,
There is not purer evil,
For he lives on it
And his name is
The King of Death.

Ronell Hatto (11)
Stamford Hill Primary School, Tottenham

The Vanishing Lady

She is a kingdom of riches
And divine beauty.

She is a concealed fire
Burning to find the light.

She is a precious jewel
Luminous to the eyes of God.

She is a lustrous green, shining effortlessly
In the never-ending sea of darkness.

Raine Mondesir-Payne (11)
Stamford Hill Primary School, Tottenham

The Last Woman In Winter

Her face is covered in pale white skin
That hid among her snow-white hair
And a neck full of hairy trees

Her face is muddled up
Like leaves in spring
Her hairy, sunny spots
Ready to burst like rain

She is an old dinosaur of many centuries
A dinosaur that has been kept in a dark cave for centuries
She is a monster full of lies
That slip out of her hairy mouth.

Simona Zivkovska (10)
Stamford Hill Primary School, Tottenham

Horror Of Sight

She is shivering like an icy crystal,
Waiting to be warmed up.
Her eyes are light blue
And they look like the deep blue sea.
She is as lonely as a stone that is locked up.
In a dark chamber full of spiders.
She's a young girl,
Looking for someone to guide her.
The sky is grey,
Waiting for the sun to pop out.
Maybe someone might come
And rescue her.

Mohamed Ahmed (10)
Stamford Hill Primary School, Tottenham

Cunningham's Daughter

Cunningham's daughter is as soft as a baby's skin,
But everyone knows how wicked she is.
She is as sweet as a rose
And as fresh as clothes out of the washing machine,
But everyone knows how evil she is.
Her hair is a long, silky, blue river, flowing down her back.
She looks like a bright gold star full of kindness and love,
But everyone knows how foul she is.
Her lips are the colour of a blood-red rose
And she is very adorable,
But everyone knows how vicious she is.
Cunningham's daughter is as soft as a baby's skin,
But everyone knows how wicked she is!

Atera Rahman (11)
Stamford Hill Primary School, Tottenham

The Girl

Her thin, red lips are shaded,
So full of secrets,
That she cannot laugh.
Her lips are as red as a strawberry,
Eyes so oval,
That she stares at people,
With horror and is too eerie to believe.
The girl's hair is as fine
As a pointy spike.
Her mouth is like an empty cave
And it will turn into a ghost train.

Lisa Thi Tran (10)
Stamford Hill Primary School, Tottenham

A Roman Soldier's Tale

I am cold,
I am hungry,
I'm miles from home,
I feel like a slave,
I am all alone.

It's hot all day long as we build Hadrian's Wall,
Stone by stone, east to west,
Day by day, not time to rest.

My body's full of pain, I'm drained, tired, I'm on my own,
I miss all my loved ones,
I want to go home.

By day we are soldiers, heroes they say,
Warriors, gods, men we should pray.
If only they knew what it's like to be me,
I'm scared and I'm homesick
Oh let me be free!

Luke Brown (10)
Ticehurst & Flimwell CE Primary School, Wadhurst

My Fat Old Guinea Pigs

Waddling around the green, grassy run,
Nestling in the golden straw,
Squeaking loudly and indignantly,
Yawning long and lazily.

They may be fat, they may be old,
They may have attitude, they may be mean,
I love my guinea pigs,
I always will.

They love the food, they hate tomatoes! *Yuck!*
Cut the talk, dish out the grub!
I love my guinea pigs,
I always will.

Emily Iliffe (10)
Ticehurst & Flimwell CE Primary School, Wadhurst

Sick Of Bricks

I am a Roman soldier and I feel so sad,
We are building Hadrian's Wall and it's driving me mad!
There is cold, crispy, cloudy weather,
These bricks are not exactly light as a feather!
I can smell smoke from a fire,
We are getting our gold tomorrow.
I feel fed up and extremely homesick,
My pals are going crazy, especially Nick.
I have got a cold coming on and my nose is red,
I feel so tired and I want to go to bed!
I feel the rough, funny shaped brick,
I am absolutely starving and I feel sick.
You know what I would rather hear the boy say,
'You're fired!' instead of, 'You're hired!'
I want to go home,
Yes Boss, that means going back to Rome!
I wonder what part of the wall I will build today?
I wonder if I will ever get my pay?

Jodie Howe (9)
Ticehurst & Flimwell CE Primary School, Wadhurst

Slow And Fast

My Dog
My dog creeping up on a cat
and suddenly up she jumps!
No more cat.

My Snake
My snake slithering up on a mouse
Snap! Squeak! No more mouse.

My Cat
My cat sneaking up on a duck
Suddenly, quack! No more duck.

Ryan Bell (9)
Ticehurst & Flimwell CE Primary School, Wadhurst

Happy, Healthy Me

H aving a birthday party with my mates.
A t the beach in the sea with my family.
P icking up my sister from school and going to my nan's.
P icking bluebells in the forest and
Y oung apples.

H aving healthy food like
E ating some
A pricots
L ight crisps and
T asty fruit and veg
H aving less fat
Y elling in the pool.

M eeting my mum for a jog
E ating my favourite food.

Clarice Wale (10)
Ticehurst & Flimwell CE Primary School, Wadhurst

Happy, Healthy Me

H aving dinner with my friends
A lso playing with my friends
P laying in the park
P laying with my dog
Y ay, it's teatime.

H aving a balanced diet
E ating healthy things
A pples are healthy
L earning all the seven food groups
T he people that don't
H ave these foods will get fat
Y ou need to eat fruit.

M mm, food
E ating too much food will make you sick.

George Thomas (8)
Ticehurst & Flimwell CE Primary School, Wadhurst

Anancy The Spider

Anancy is a spider
Who is very wise.
He has eight legs
And only two eyes.

Anancy has a drum
And also two hats.
He sometimes get the better of people
Even the biggest cats.

Anancy stays in a hot, steamy jungle
He tricks animals when the time is right.
He relaxes on his ubuluembu most of the day and night.

When the slaves were taken to Jamaica
To serve their masters,
They were tired, hungry, sad and homesick
And their leaders were getting nastier.

Amy-Lee Fisher (10)
Ticehurst & Flimwell CE Primary School, Wadhurst

The Pineapple

Golden, yellow, spiky diamonds
glistening on the rocky skin.
I can hear the succulent juices
as I cut its fleshy surface.
My nose wrinkles when the
sweet-smelling fragrance
drifts slowly through the air.
Sticky, prickly, squashy
as I touch this beautiful fruit.
My mouth waters when I eat
this juicy, sweet, tropical treat.
A pineapple is truly scrumptious.

Eleanor Sands (9)
Ticehurst & Flimwell CE Primary School, Wadhurst

The Sizzling Sausage

My favourite food is long and spicy,
I can hear it sizzling in the pan.

My nose wrinkles with the smell,
My taste buds are saying, 'We want it now!'

It tastes so good, I can't wait,
It feels so wobbly to touch.

My favourite food is sausages,
I just love them so much.

Aaron Mills (9)
Ticehurst & Flimwell CE Primary School, Wadhurst

Parrot

I've got a lazy old parrot
Who eats a lot but doesn't sleep
He lets you stroke him if you know him
But then, you go to stroke him and . . .
Snap!
Your finger's gone!
One down, nine more to go!

Billie-Jean Stacy (9)
Ticehurst & Flimwell CE Primary School, Wadhurst

Frog

Zap, out goes tongue!
Fast!
Splash in the pond.
Jump out!
Stretch your long, bony, green legs
And move your eyes round in a circle.

Jasmine Perry (10)
Ticehurst & Flimwell CE Primary School, Wadhurst

My Usual Day

Monday to Sunday
Sun up to sundown
'Lift, move faster!' I hear them scream
Will my feet keep up?
It's hot, I can't move
Bang on my back, it is burning badly
No water to soothe
On goes the sack
My legs go weak
My head feels heavy
Pull, pull, pull
Again and again
My biggest fear of danger
To wake up again.

Amber Brooker (10)
Ticehurst & Flimwell CE Primary School, Wadhurst

Blood And Sweat

Crack
'Work faster!'
Clank go our spades on rocks
My back hurts,
My fingers bleed,
My legs ache,
I am cold and tired.
It's hard work building this wall,
I hope I get my pay
At the end of the day.

Joshua Grinham (9)
Ticehurst & Flimwell CE Primary School, Wadhurst

Another Day

Another day at Hadrian's Wall,
God I wish I wasn't here at all.
They make us work so hard and fast,
This is such an awful task.
We work through wind and rain,
This wall is such a pain.
We get fed once a day
And do not receive any pay.
Another day at Hadrian's Wall.

Gemma West (10)
Ticehurst & Flimwell CE Primary School, Wadhurst

A Cold Roman Soldier

I am a cold Roman soldier building a wall
With no cover from the rain, I'm frozen to the bone
I miss my wife and children, they are at home
Where the olive trees grow in the hot sun all day long.
Tell me why we need this wall,
To the empire it is all,
But to me it is nothing.

Edward Bennett (10)
Ticehurst & Flimwell CE Primary School, Wadhurst

Winter

The crisp snow glistens like diamonds in the sun's fiery shadow.
Trees stand naked, stripped of their golden leaves.
The ground is invisible, masked in a cloak of ice and snow.
The icy winds blow like tornadoes, sweeping up the remaining leaves
and capturing them.
The lakes and tarns freeze, trapping underneath a majestic
carpet of water.
Here the winter's true magic is displayed.

Charles Winstanley (11)
Trawden Primary School, Colne

The Smell Of Roses

The smell of roses,
The smell of trees,
The smell of everything
Is fine for me.

The smell of fresh bread,
The smell of wheat,
The smell of everything,
Is good for me.

The smell of cakes,
The smell of sweets,
The smell of everything,
Is great for me.

The smell of wood,
The smell of grass,
The smell of everything,
Is brill for me.

Laura Hawken (8)
Whitemoor Primary School, St Austell

Elephants

I can see a trunk.
I can see big ears.
I can see a short tail
I can see four feet.
I can see some slow ones.
I can see some fast ones.
I can see a fat tummy.
I can see a young one.
I can see a little one.
I can see some big toenails.
I can see a big mouth.
I love elephants.

Brendan Collings (7)
Whitemoor Primary School, St Austell

I Can See

I can see a long stem
I can see some nice pollen
I can see a prickly leaf
I can see a long root
I can see an orange petal
I can see a yellow colour
I can see a smooth leaf
I can see a little petal
I can see a beautiful flower.

Fiona Hawkey (8)
Whitemoor Primary School, St Austell

Stars

I can see a shining moon
Like the stars in the sky
Twinkling high above my head
Twirling, twisting, faster than a roundabout.
I can see amazing planets
Circling above me very far away.

Shakkira Perryman (7)
Whitemoor Primary School, St Austell

On My Bike

On my bike . . .
Going to the park on my bike
My bike has hard brakes.
I can do wheelies on my bike
My bike can do jumps.

Luke Harby (6)
Whitemoor Primary School, St Austell

Love

Love is dark purple
Love is plants
Love is friends that care
Love is happiness
Love is a present
Love is a family
Love is love and compassion
Love is poems.

Sadie Firkins (8)
Whitemoor Primary School, St Austell

Lions

I can imagine lions growling,
I can imagine lions fighting,
I can imagine lions' prey,
I can imagine lions killing.
I can imagine lion cubs playing rough and tumble,
I can imagine lions' manes,
I can imagine lionesses licking their lion cubs,
Lions are my favourite animals.

Ben Hooper (7)
Whitemoor Primary School, St Austell

High Peaks

High peaks
K2 has snow on top
Everest is the peak where climbers climb
Shafil Pike the tall peak of England
Ben Nevis, tall but cold
Pointy, nearly as high as Everest.

Marcus Reed (7)
Whitemoor Primary School, St Austell

Tigers

I can see some black stripes,
I can see a sea of orange,
I can see some fierce eyes,
I can see a wagging tail,
I can see some tiger cubs,
I can see a white tummy,
I can see two flapping ears,
I can see a group of tigers,
I can see a black nose,
I can see a stripy body,
I can see six whiskers.
Tigers are the best.

Steven Mclinden (6)
Whitemoor Primary School, St Austell

Happy

When I play with Sassy it makes me happy
When I watch my favourite programme it makes me happy
When I play with my best friend it makes me happy
When I play games it makes me happy.
Being happy is fun!

Ebony Uren (7)
Whitemoor Primary School, St Austell

Pony Poem

I can see a mane
I can see a bridle shining in the sun
I can see some mud as wet as the rain
I can see two blue eyes looking at me
I love ponies.

Lauren Parish (7)
Whitemoor Primary School, St Austell

I Can See A Picture

I can see a man
Feeding a cat milk
I can see a washing line
I can see a steaming pot of soup
I can see an old fire stove
I can see a patchwork cushion
I can see a long, grey beard and hair
I can see the mouse hole and the cat.

Sophie Symons (7)
Whitemoor Primary School, St Austell

Going On My Bike

On my bike I like to go round the garden
It is bright red and shiny
On my bike I zoom around and around
It has giant wheels
On my bike I do amazing wheelies
It is very tall
On my bike I have lots of fun.

Jowan Dorson (6)
Whitemoor Primary School, St Austell

My Sasha

My Sasha is grey, black and white
My Sasha loves to play with Brandy
My Sasha's teeth are like needles
My Sasha's coat is soft
My Sasha loves to play outside with us.

Katie Parish (6)
Whitemoor Primary School, St Austell

My Classroom

I can see brown hair,
I can see a green pencil case,
I can see spiky hair,
I can see posters,
I can see a skipping rope,
I can see an alphabet,
I can see Nemo,
I can see a chair,
I can see a classroom,
I can see some stars,
I can see a computer.
This is my friendly classroom.

Rebecca Manship (7)
Whitemoor Primary School, St Austell

My Dream

In my dream I can fly up high
In my dream I can walk the skies
In my dream I can touch the sun
In my dream it is such fun.

In my bed peaceful and calm
I dream of monsters, adventures and much more.
In my dream I can travel the world
In my dream it is marvellous fun.

Alex John (9)
Ysgol Glannau Gwaun, Fishguard